RELIGIOUS EDUCATION IN THE PUBLIC SCHOOLS OF THE STATE AND CITY OF NEW YORK

A HISTORICAL STUDY

A DISSERTATION

SUBMITTED TO THE FACULTY OF THE GRADUATE SCHOOL OF ARTS AND LITERATURE IN CANDIDACY FOR THE DEGREE OF DOCTOR OF PHILOSOPHY

(THE GRADUATE DIVINITY SCHOOL: RELIGIOUS EDUCATION)

BY

ARTHUR JACKSON HALL

THE UNIVERSITY OF CHICAGO PRESS
CHICAGO, ILLINOIS

The University of Chicago

RELIGIOUS EDUCATION IN THE PUBLIC SCHOOLS OF THE STATE AND CITY OF NEW YORK

A HISTORICAL STUDY

A DISSERTATION

SUBMITTED TO THE FACULTY OF THE GRADUATE SCHOOL OF ARTS AND LITERATURE IN CANDIDACY FOR THE DEGREE OF DOCTOR OF PHILOSOPHY

(THE GRADUATE DIVINITY SCHOOL: RELIGIOUS EDUCATION)

BY
ARTHUR JACKSON HALL

THE UNIVERSITY OF CHICAGO PRESS
CHICAGO, ILLINOIS

Published June 1914

Composed and Printed By
The University of Chicago Press
Chicago, Illinois, U.S.A.

TO

MY FATHER AND MOTHER

WHO FIRST LED ME IN THE WAY
OF KNOWLEDGE AND

TO

MY WIFE

THE INSPIRATION OF AFTER YEARS

CONTENTS

PAGE

Bibliography vii

PART I

CHAPTER

I. Education under the Dutch Régime 3

II. Education under the English Régime 10

III. Education under the Auspices of the Society for the Propagation of the Gospel 16

IV. Educational Movements of the Early Nineteenth Century 21

V. Elementary-School Books of the Eighteenth Century . 26

PART II

VI. The Rising Consciousness of Sectarianism in Education . 39

VII. The Final Legal Status of Sectarian Instruction . . 48

VIII. The Religious Conception of Education in Process of Modification 63

IX. The Reading of the Bible in the Public Schools . . 73

X. The Philosophic Aspects of the Question 95

BIBLIOGRAPHY

I. REFERENCES TO ORIGINAL MATERIAL

Albany Records. Consulted for this thesis only as quoted in Pratt's *Annals.*

An Honest Appeal to Every Voter. Pamphlet, Public Library, New York City.

Arguments, Points, and Amendments of N. G. Green to Proposed Education Law before New York Legislature, 1899, on behalf of Catholic interests of the State of New York.

Barnard, *American Journal of Education.*

Brinsly, *Ludus Literarius.*

Clews, Elsie, *Educational Legislation and Administration of the Colonial Governments.*

Coote, *English School-Master.*

Debate on Amendment *re* Religious Instruction in Free Schools and Charitable Institutions. *Revised Record of Constitutional Convention,* 1894, V, 3, 959–86.

Decision of the State Superintendent of Common Schools on the Right to Compel Catholic Children to Attend Prayers, etc. Pamphlet, Public Library, New York City.

Dilworth's *Speller,* ed. 1771.

Evans, *American Bibliography.*

Fernow, Berthold, *Records of New Amsterdam from 1653–1674.*

Hasse, *Index to Documents of the State of New York.*

Hastings, *Ecclesiastical Records of New York.*

Hoole, "The New Discovery of the Old Art of Teaching," *Barnard's Journal,* V, 17.

Laws of the State of New York, especially for the years 1842, 1843, 1844, 1851, 1871, 1897, 1901.

Memorials, Petitions, Pamphlets, Speeches, etc.

Minutes of Common Council of City of New York.

New England Primer, reprint of ed. 1777.

New York City: *Report of the Commissioners of the Public School Money for 1841.* Pamphlet, Public Library, New York City.

New York City: *Report of the Committee . . . . Relative to the Use of the Bible in the Public Schools of the City.* Pamphlet, Public Library, New York City.

O'Callaghan, E. B., *Documents Relative to the Colonial History of the State of New York, Procured by J. R. Brodhead.*

———, *Laws and Ordinances of New Netherland.* 1638–74.

———, *Register of New Netherland.* 1626–74.

Pettis, S., *An Address from an Instructor to His Scholars; Pronounced at Woodstock, April 14, 1804.*

Pratt, *Annals of Public Education in the State of New York from 1626–1746.*

Preston, "What the Catholics Want," *Forum*, V, 1.

Proceedings of the Board of Aldermen, New York City.

Proceedings of the Board of Assistants, New York City.

Public School Society—Annual Reports.

Records of New Amsterdam, 1653–1674.

Report on Petition of Certain Roman Catholics of New York, Utica, Syracuse, etc., *re* Instruction of Their Children, Assembly Document 97, 1853, V, 4.

Reports of State Superintendent of Public Instruction.

Savage, J. W., *Remarks in Assembly, April 5, 1854, upon the Bill "Amending the Common School Law" so That No Part of the Common School Fund Shall Be Appropriated to the Support of Sectarian Schools*, etc. Pamphlet, Public Library, New York City.

The Legislature of New York Hoodwinked by the Romanists. 1858. Pamphlet, Public Library, New York City.

Van Laer, A. J. F., New York. *Van Rensselaer Bowier Manuscripts.*

Walsh, "Religious Education in the Public Schools of Massachusetts," *American Catholic Quarterly Review*, V, 29.

II. REFERENCES TO SECONDARY MATERIAL

Brodhead, J. R., *History of the State of New York.* First Period 1609–64.

"Bible Reading in the Public Schools in the United States," *Report of U.S. Commissioner of Education 1897–98*, V, II, p. 1539.

Bluntschli, *Theory of the State.*

Bolton, *History of the Church in Westchester County.*

Bourne, *History of the Public School Society.*

Brown, E. E., *The Making of Our Middle Schools.*

Bushnell, H., *Common Schools; Discourse on the Modifications Demanded by the Roman Catholics.* 1853.

Butler, N. M., "Religious Instruction and Its Relation to Education," *Educational Review*, V, 18, p. 425.

Butler, Nathaniel, "The Moral and Religious Element in Education," *Religious Education*, V, I, pp. 88 f.

Central Conference of American Rabbis. *Why the Bible Should Not Be Read in the Public Schools.* New York, 1906, Bloch Publishing Co.

Cheever, G. B., *Right of the Bible in Our Public Schools.* 1854.

Clark, R. W., *The Question of the Hour: the Bible and the School Fund.* 1870.

Coe, G. A., "Moral and Religious Education from the Psychological Point of View," *Religious Education*, V, III, pp. 165 f.

Colwell, S., *The Position of Christianity in the U.S., in Its Relations with Our Political Institutions*, etc. 1854.

Cooley, *Constitutional Limitations*, 2d ed.

Crooker, J. H., "Moral and Religious Instruction in our Public Schools," *Problems in American Society*. 1889.

De Garmo, "Present Status of Religious Instruction in England, France, Germany, and the United States," *Christian Knowledge Lectures*. 1900.

Dorchester, D., *Romanism versus the Public School System*. 1888.

Dunshee, *History of the School of the Reformed Protestant Dutch Church in the City of New York*.

Durant, H. F., *Defence of the Use of the Bible in the Common Schools*, etc. 1859.

Dutton, S. T., "Religious and Ethical Influences of the Public School," *Religious Education*, V, I, pp. 47 f.

Earle, *Child Life in Colonial Days*.

Eggleston, *The Transit of Civilization*.

Fisher, G. P., "Cardinal Manning and Public Schools," *Forum*, V, VII, pp. 119 f.

Fitch, C. E., *The Public School. History of Common School Education in New York from 1633–1904*.

Ford, *The New England Primer*.

Gibbons, J., Cardinal, and others, "Two Sides of the School Question," *Proceedings of N.E.A.*, 1889, pp. 111 f.

Hawks, F. L., *Contributions to the Ecclesiastical History of the United States of America*.

Hecker, "Catholics and Protestants Agreeing on the School Question," *Catholic World*, February, 1881.

Henry, J., *An Address upon Education and Common Schools, Delivered at Cooperstown, Ostego Co., September 21, 1843*. Public Library, New York City.

Humphreys, *Gospel in North America*.

Hurlbut, E. P., *A Secular View of Religion in the State, and the Bible in the Public Schools*. 1870.

Johnson, *Old-Time Schools and School-Books*.

Littlefield, *Early Schools and School-Books of New England*.

MacQuary, H., "The Bible in the Public Schools," in his *Topics of the Times*. 1891.

Manning, Cardinal, "The Bible in the Public Schools," *Forum*, V, VIII, pp. 52 f.

Mayo, A. D., *What Does the Bible Represent in the American Common School?* 1874.

Mayo, A. D., and Vickers, T., *The Bible in the Public Schools*. 1st ed. 1870.

Mead, E. A., *The Function of the Public Schools in the Scheme of Human Welfare*.

Meriwether, *Our Colonial Curriculum*.

Mott, T. A., "The Church and the Public School," *Proceedings of N.E.A.*, 1901.

O'Callaghan, *Laws and Ordinances of New Netherland*. 1638–74.

———, *History of New Netherland*.

Palmer, A. E., *The New York Public School.*
Patton, W. W., *Purely Secular Public Schools; Address on the Bible and Public Schools, September 24, 1876.*
Politics and the School Question; Attitude of the Republican and Democratic Parties. 1876.
Prince, J. F., "The Bible in Education," *Educational Review*, 1898.
Randall, *History of the Common School System of the State of New York.*
Spear, S. T., *Religion and the State, or, The Bible and the Public Schools.*
Strong, Josiah, *Religion and the Public Schools.* Pamphlet, Congregational Sunday School Publishing Society.
Strong, T. M., *The History of the Town of Flatbush.*
"The Bible in the Schools," *The Nation*, November 18, 1869; January 6, 1870; February 17, 1870.
Thiry, J. H., *History of the Early Schools in Long Island.* 1904.
Thomson, J. P., *Shall Our Common Schools Be Destroyed?* 1870. Pamphlet, Public Library, New York City.
Tuer, *History of the Horn-Book.*
Tufts, J. H., "Moral Training in the Public Schools," *Religious Education*, V, III, pp. 125 f.
Ullman, D., *Amendments to the Constitution of the United States.* 1876. Pamphlet, Public Library, New York City.
Van Vechter, E., *Early Schools and Schoolmasters of New Amsterdam.*
Watson, F., *The English Grammar Schools to 1660: Their Curriculum and Practice.*
Wilson, R. R., *New York; Old and New. Its Story, Streets, and Landmarks.*
Woolsey, *Political Science.*

III. STATE SUPREME COURT DECISIONS ON BIBLE READING AND RELIGIOUS EXERCISES IN THE PUBLIC SCHOOLS

Maine Decision. 1854. *Maine Reports*, 38, pp. 379–413.
Massachusetts Decision. 1866. *Massachusetts Reports*, 12 Allen, 127.
Ohio Decision. 1872. *Ohio Reports*, 23, pp. 211–54.
Iowa Decision. 1884. *Iowa Reports*, 54, pp. 367–70.
Wisconsin Decision. 1890. *Wisconsin Reports*, 76, pp. 177–221.
Michigan Decision. 1898. *Michigan Reports*, 118, pp. 560–95.
Nebraska Decision. 1902. *Nebraska Reports*, 65, pp. 853–85.
Kansas Decision. 1904. *Kansas Reports*, 69, pp. 53–58.
Kentucky Decision. 1905. *Kentucky Reports*, 120, pp. 608–31.
Texas Decision. 1908. *L.R.A.* (N.S.), 8960; 109 *S. W. Reports*, 115.
Illinois Decision. 1910. *Illinois Reports*, 245, pp. 334–78; cf. 93 Ill. 61; 95 Ill. 263; 137 Ill. 296; 121 Ill. 297.

PART I

RELIGIOUS EDUCATION INCORPORATED IN THE SCHOOLS

CHAPTER I

EDUCATION UNDER THE DUTCH RÉGIME

There can be no reason to suppose that the conception of education entertained by the Dutch colonists in New Netherland was any different from that which prevailed in the Fatherland. The country alone was new; the people and their modes of thinking still belonged to the old world. The founders of New Amsterdam had brought with them the institutions of their native land. We are justified therefore in going back to Holland for our introduction to Dutch education in America. Only a few years before the colonists inaugurated their first school the Synod of Dort, held in 1618–19, had given expression to the settled conviction of the Dutch mind respecting the education of youth, an opinion which had been slowly maturing since the beginning of the Reformation. One of the resolutions on this subject, passed November 30, 1618, reads as follows: "Schools, in which the young shall be properly instructed in the principles of Christian doctrine shall be instituted not only in cities, but also in towns and country places where heretofore none have existed. The Christian magistracy shall be requested that well-qualified persons may be employed and enabled to devote themselves to the service; and especially that the children of the poor may be gratuitously instructed, and not be excluded from the benefit of the schools. In this office none shall be employed but such as are members of the Reformed church, having certificates of an upright faith and pious life, and of being well versed in the truths of the Catechism. They are to sign a document, professing their belief in the Confession of Faith and the Heidelberg Catechism, and promising that they will give catechetical instruction to the youth in the principles of Christian truth according to the same. The schoolmasters shall instruct their scholars according to their age and capacity, at least two days in the week, not only by causing them to commit to memory, but also by instilling in their minds an acquaintance with the truths of the Catechism. . . . . The schoolmasters shall take care not only that the scholars commit these catechisms to memory, but that they suitably understand the doctrines contained in them. For this purpose, they shall suitably explain to everyone, in a manner adapted to his capacity, and frequently inquire if they understand them. The schoolmasters shall bring every one of the pupils committed to their charge to the hearing of the preached Word, and particularly the preaching on the Catechism, and require from them an account of the same" (quoted in Dunshee, 2d ed., p. 4. For full titles of sources see special bibliography).

The Synod of Dort, whose Canons were everywhere accepted by the Dutch people as one of the symbols of their faith, thus provided for the religious education of children and youth. Religion and education were considered inseparable. "The principles of Christian doctrine" were to be an essential and indispensable part of the subject-matter of instruction. We shall now proceed to show how this conception of education was brought over into the new world and incorporated in the schools set up by the Dutch in the colony of New Netherland. The accessible data on this topic fall into two general classes: the religious motive in education, and religious material in education.

The motive that actuated the Dutch colonists may be seen, first, in the stipulations of official documents. In the charter of freedoms and exemptions granted by the West India Company, June 7, 1629, to all patroons, masters, or private persons who should plant colonies in New Netherland, the following condition is specified: "The Patroons and colonists shall in particular, and in the speediest manner, endeavor to find out ways and means whereby they may supply a minister and schoolmaster, that thus the service of God and zeal for religion may not grow cool and be neglected among them" (*N.Y. Col. Doc.*, II, 557). With a few verbal changes the same decree was re-enacted in the freedoms and exemptions of 1630 (*N.Y.*, *Col. Doc.* I, 99).

In consequence of disagreement between the Nine Men and the Director, in 1649, the former presented a memorial and remonstrance to the States-General of Holland, setting forth "the reasons and cause of the great decay of New Netherland," and "in what manner New Netherland should be relieved." Under the latter head is found the following complaint: "There ought to be also a public school provided with at least two good teachers, so that the youth, in so wild a country, where there are so many dissolute people, may, first of all, be well instructed and indoctrinated not only in reading and writing, but also in the knowledge and fear of the Lord" (*N.Y. Col. Doc.*, I, 317).

The religious motive in education is also seen in a civil ordinance relative to the public catechizing of the children in the church, passed by the Director-General and Council, March 17, 1664: "Whereas, it is highly necessary and of great consequence that the youth, from their childhood, is well instructed in reading, writing and arithmetic, and principally in the principles and fundaments of the Christian religion . . . . so that in time such men may arise from it, who may be able to serve their country in Church or in State . . . . they [Director-General and Council] have deemed it necessary to recommend the present schoolmaster, and to command him, so as it is done by this, that they (Pietersen, the Principal, and Van Hoboecken, of the branch school on the Bouwery) on Wednesday, before the beginning of the sermon, with the children intrusted to their care, shall appear in the Church to examine, after the close of the sermon, each of them his own scholars, in the presence of the reverend ministers and elders who may there be present, what they, in the course of the week, do remember of the Christian commands and catechism, and what progress they have made" (O'Call., *Laws of N.N.*, 461; Dunshee, p. 30).

In the next place, the religious motive in education is seen in the requirement that all teachers be licensed by the civil and ecclesiastical authorities (Pratt's *Ann.*, p. 69). In support of this proposition are offered the following extracts from the original records:

"On motion—the Attorney-General is commanded, to go to the house of Jacob Van Corler [Corlear], who has, since some time, arrogated to himself to keep school, and to warn him that Director-General and Council have deemed it proper to send him a *supersedeas* till he shall have solicited and obtained from the Director-General and Council an act in *propria forma.* 19 February, 1658" (*Alb. Rec.*, XIV, 114; quoted in Pratt's *Ann.*, p. 19).

"In Council, 19 March, 1658

"Presented a petition of burgomasters and schepens of this city, soliciting, that Jacob Van Corlear, who, on the 19 February last, was interdicted by the Director-General and Council to keep school, might be permitted it in the city. The apostil was—

"School-keeping and the appointment of schoolmasters depend absolutely from the *jus Patronatus* in virtue of which Director-General and Council interdicted school-keeping to Jacob Van Corlear, as having arrogated it to himself without their orders, in which resolution they do as yet persist" (*Alb. Rec.*, XIV, 151; quoted in Pratt's *Ann.*, p. 20).

"Andreas Hudde appeared before the Director-General and Council, and solicited a license to keep school, received for answer that the Council shall ask upon his proposal the opinion of the Minister and the Consistory. Done in New Amsterdam, 31 December, 1665" (*Alb. Rec.*, IX, 309; quoted in Pratt's *Ann.*, p. 19).

After the capitulation of New Amsterdam the government of the province passed into the hands of the English. The Dutch people, however, still remained in the country and kept up their church and their school. By the articles of capitulation they were allowed "the liberty of their consciences in divine worship and church discipline, with all their accustomed jurisdiction with respect to the poor and orphans" (O'Call., *Hist. N.N.*, II, 533). This privilege was ratified by William III (charter of incorporation of the Dutch church, 1696), with the plain specification that the minister and deacons should have the right to nominate and appoint a schoolmaster and such other officers as might be needed by the congregation over which they presided (Dunshee, p. 37). Notwithstanding, the English governors attempted to assert their authority and to prevent any Dutch minister or schoolmaster from exercising his calling "without a special gubernatorial license" (Dunshee, p. 37). Lord Cornbury succeeded in breaking up the Dutch schools on Long Island, and, with like intent, proceeded against the school of the Dutch church in New York City. But this was a strong and influential congregation, and so the Governor's attempt was stoutly and successfully resisted. The subsequent minutes bearing on the subject are lacking, until January 5, 1726. At that time the Consistory engaged Barent de Foreest to give "instruction not only in the Low Dutch language, but also in the elements of Christian piety" (Dunshee, p. 38). The contention of the Dutch for the right to appoint their own schoolmasters can be assigned probably to no other reason than their unwillingness to have their children brought under the influence of the Church of England, and their settled determination to have them indoctrinated in the principles of the Reformed faith. This no doubt explains the requirement under the Dutch régime that all schoolmasters be licensed by the civil and ecclesiastical authorities.

Again, the religious motive in education is seen in the character and qualifications demanded of schoolmasters. Director Stuyvesant wrote to the Classis of Amsterdam "for a pious, well-qualified and diligent schoolmaster." In response to this request the Directors of the West India Company wrote, February 16, 1650: "We appoint, at your request, a schoolmaster, who shall also act as comforter for the sick. He is considered an honest and pious man, and shall embark at the first opportunity." On April 15 of the same year the Directors wrote: "The schoolmaster for whom you solicited comes in the same vessel with this letter. The Lord grant that he may for a long time exemplify the favorable testimony which he carried with him from here, to the edification of the youth" (*Alb. Rec.*, IV, 23, 30; quoted in Pratt's *Ann.*, p. 10).

From a letter by the Directors of the West India Company to Peter Stuyvesant, May 2, 1661, announcing the appointment of Evert Pietersen schoolmaster in New Amsterdam, is taken the following extract: "Whereas, we have deemed it necessary to promote religious worship, and to read to the inhabitants the word of God, to exhort them, to lead them in the ways of the Lord, and console the sick, that an expert person was sent to New Netherland, in the city of New Amsterdam, who at the same time should act there as chorister and schoolmaster; so it is, that we, upon the good report which we have received about the person of Evert Pietersen, and confiding in his abilities and experience in the aforesaid services, together on his pious character and virtues, have, on your Honor's recommendation, and that of the magistrates of the city of New Amsterdam, appointed the aforesaid person as consoler of the sick, chorister and schoolmaster, at New Amsterdam, in New Netherland, which charge he shall fulfil there, and conduct himself in these with all diligence and faithfulness; also we expect that he shall give others a good example, so as it becomes a pious and good consoler, clerk, chorister and schoolmaster" (*Alb. Rec.*, VIII, 321; quoted in Pratt's *Ann.*, p. 18). Besides bringing into prominence the "pious character and virtues" of the said Evert Pietersen as a condition of his appointment to the school in New Amsterdam the foregoing extract enumerates the other offices with which the schoolmaster of that period was almost uniformly burdened, all of which in their turn required that he be a man of religious disposition. It was demanded of the schoolmaster that he be a man of pious character because it was deemed "necessary to promote religious worship, and to read to the inhabitants the word of God," etc.

Religious material in education finds abundant illustration in the subject-matter of instruction. The following extracts are offered in support of this proposition:

Articles of agreement with Johannes Van Eckkelen, accepted schoolmaster and chorister of Flatbush, 1682: "II. When the school begins, one of the children shall read the morning prayer, as it stands in the catechism, and close with the prayer before dinner; in the afternoon it shall begin with the prayer after dinner, and end with the evening prayer. The evening school shall begin with the Lord's Prayer, and close by singing a psalm.

"III. He shall instruct the children on every Wednesday and Saturday in the common prayers, and the questions and answers in the catechism, to enable them to repeat them the better on Sunday before the afternoon service, or on Monday, when they shall be catechized before the congregation" (Strong's *History of Flatbush*, p. 111). Practically this same agreement was made nearly one hundred years later, 1773, by the town of Flatbush with one Anthony Welp (Strong's *History of Flatbush*, p. 115).

In January, 1726, Barent de Foreest was engaged schoolmaster for the Collegiate Dutch Church, New York City. By agreement "the school was to be opened and closed with prayer and singing, and the children, according to their capacity, were to be taught to spell and read and write and cipher, and also the usual prayers in the catechism.

"On Saturday morning they were to be prepared to repeat to the minister the Lord's-Day portion in the catechism, which was to be subject of discourse the following day, so as to be able to recite it in the church.

"Every Monday the scholars were to be publicly catechized—and on Wednesdays, when there was preaching, he and the scholars were to come to church in a body.

. . . .

"None but edifying and orthodox textbooks were to be used, such as would meet with the approbation of the Reverend Consistory" (Dunshee, p. 39).

In 1733, Gerrit Van Wagenen became the successor to Barent de Foreest. By the terms of agreement he was required to teach "the principles of the true Reformed religion," "the usual prayers and the Heidelberg Catechism" (Dunshee, p. 43).

In 1810, James Forester entered upon his duties as master of the school of the Collegiate Church. He was to teach among other things reading in the New Testament, the Old Testament, and the Heidelberg Catechism (Dunshee, p. 71).

Henry Onderdonk, Jr., a New York historian of the first half of the nineteenth century, describes the Dutch primers as follows: "Religion was the leading idea in Dutch teaching. I have a Dutch Primer, or A.B.C. Book, as it is called (Amsterdam), similar to our New England Primer. It has a large rooster on one page, and a picture of a Dutch school on the other. The master has a cap on his head and a bunch of twigs in his hand. The class stands before him and the other boys are seated at their desks. After a very little spelling, succeeds the Lord's Prayer, Creed, Decalogue, Morning and Evening Prayer, Grace before and after meat. The instruction is altogether religious, which feature (I suppose) is retained in our Catholic schools to this day" (Pratt's *Ann.*, p. 117).

The religious element in Dutch education is therefore clearly seen, on the side of motive, in the stipulations of official documents, in the licensing of schoolmasters, and in the character and qualifications demanded of teachers; on the side of material, it finds sufficient and conclusive illustration in the subject-matter of instruction.

CHAPTER II

EDUCATION UNDER THE ENGLISH RÉGIME

The English people had known no other kind of education than religious. Prior to the Reformation education was by the church and for the church. The Reformation, so far as concerns education, had merely transferred the seat of authority from the pope and his bishops to the king and his bishops. The school became one of the strong arms of Protestantism and one of the principal means of popularizing the new propaganda.

During the first half of the seventeenth century the Bible formed the center of instruction. By the more advanced pupils it was to be read in Greek and Hebrew, as well as in English. It was also used devotionally every morning at the opening, and every afternoon at the close, of school. Care was also taken to instruct the children in the doctrinal grounds of religion, and for this purpose the Catechism, the Creed, the Ten Commandments, and the Lord's Prayer were called into requisition (Watson, *The English Grammar Schools to 1660*, chaps. i–iv).

The principal pedagogical writers of this period were John Brinsly and Charles Hoole. They may be relied upon to represent the ideals, as well as the practice of the best sort of schoolmasters of their time. John Brinsly wrote his *Ludus Literarius, or The Grammar School*, in 1612. According to the title-page (2d ed., 1627), his object was to show "how to proceede from the first entrance into learning, to the highest perfection required in the Grammar Schools." The *Psalms in Meter* is recommended as one of the first reading books for children (p. 17); the pupil should not be allowed to enter the grammar school until able to read perfectly the New Testament in English (p. 13); and a knowledge of Greek and Hebrew is strongly commended, because it will enable its possessor to read the Bible in the original (pp. 223, 244). The special fitness of the New Testament as an introduction to the Greek language is urged, because it was written by the Lord himself, both in matter and words, and because, together with the Old Testament, it constitutes the Book of books and gives men the opportunity of seeing with their own eyes rather than to rest upon the assurances of others (p. 226).

Chap. xxii has the following title: "Of knowledge of the grounds of Religion and training up the schollers therein." The first paragraph thus sets forth the author's view: "Now that we have thus gone thorow all the way of learning, for whatsoever can be required in the Grammar schooles; and how to lay a sure foundation, both for the Greeke and the Hebrew, that they may be able to go on of themselves in all these by their own studies: it remaineth that we come yet to one further point, and which is as it were the end of all these. That is, how schollers may be seasoned and trained up in Gods true Religion and in grace; without which all other learning is meerely vaine, or to increase a greater condemnation. This one alone doth make them truely blessed, and sanctifie all other their studies" (p. 253).

In carrying out the view just set forth, children are to be instructed in "all the grounds of religion and chiefe Histories of the Bible," and the substance, doctrines, proofs, and uses of the sermons (p. 253; references from ed. of 1627).

But greater still, perhaps, was the influence of Charles Hoole upon the education of his time. *The Usher's Duty* and *The New Discovery of the Old Art of Teaching* were composed by him in 1637, and, together with a little pamphlet on *The Petty Schools*, were published in 1659 (Barnard's *Journal of Education*, XVII, 191; entire work reprinted in vol. XVII of this *Journal*).

On the founding of "Petty Schools," Hoole says: "The Petty School is the place where, indeed, the first principles of all religion and learning ought to be taught" (*ibid.*, XVII, 204).

Under "How a child may be taught to read any English book perfectly," Hoole says, "in order to hold to the sure foundation of religious instruction, I have caused the Lord's Prayer, the Creed, and the Ten Commandments to be printed in the Roman character, that a child having learned already to know his letters and how to spell, may also be initiated to read by them, which he will do the more cheerfully if he be also instructed at home to say them by heart" (*ibid.*, XVII, 202).

The whole school is to be divided into four forms, or grades. The lessons of the first form are to be in the Primer. The second form, learning to spell, is to be instructed from *The Single Psalter*. The third form, learning to read, has its lessons in the Bible. The fourth form is to be instructed from such "profitable English books" as may be suggested by the master and provided by the parents (*ibid.*, XVII, 205).

On the afternoons of Tuesdays and Thursdays, and on Saturday mornings, the master must hear his pupils recite "the graces, prayers and psalms, and especially the Lord's Prayer, the Creed, and the Ten Commandments (which are for that purpose set down in the New

Primer) very perfectly by heart." When these have been mastered, the pupils may proceed to other catechisms, but they must be "such as agree with the principles of Christian religion" (*ibid.*, XVII, 206).

Hoole now passes on to discuss education in the higher grades. When children, who are imperfect in reading English, are brought to the grammar school, this defect may be overcome by having them read a chapter every morning and noon in the New Testament. Also to help their memories at this time they may be required to commit parts of such psalms as the master thinks suitable to their "shallow apprehensions" (*ibid.*, XVII, 225).

Schools of the fourth form come under the instruction of the master. In the lower forms the pupils have been under the usher. The master must be careful to keep, as well as diligent to add to, what has been acquired. In order to do this, "Every morning read six to ten verses (as formerly) out of the Latin Testament into English, that thus they may become well acquainted with the matter and words of that most Holy Book; and after they are acquainted with the Greek Testament, they may proceed with it in like manner" (*ibid.*, XVII, 267).

The fifth and sixth forms are to read daily a dozen verses out of the Greek Testament.

The section on "The Master's Method" concludes by asking the blessing of God upon the teacher's planting and watering so that our young plants may grow up in "all godliness and good learning, and abound in the knowledge of our Lord Jesus Christ, whom only to know is eternal life" (*ibid.*, XVII, 282).

Chap. vii of *Scholastic Discipline* has the following title: "Of exercising scholars in the Scriptures. Of using daily prayers and singing psalms. Of taking notes at sermons, and examination after sermons."

Besides reading part of a Latin or Greek chapter, prescribed in all the forms, an English chapter was to be read every morning and night. This exercise was to be performed by one of the boys and followed by the others in their English or Latin Bibles. After the reading they were to sing a psalm in Latin, then repeat the admonitions at the end of Nowel's Catechism, concluding the whole with a prayer.

It is recommended that the master meet his pupils at school every Lord's day in the morning about an hour before church time, and instruct them in the doctrines of the catechism, and, after a psalm sung and prayer said, attend them to church. After the sermon they are to return to the school again, when the pupils are to be questioned on what they have heard of the sermon. The day's exercise is to be concluded "with the singing of a psalm and devout prayers, and charging your scholars to spend the rest of the time in reading the Scriptures and such religious books as tend to their further profiting in Christian piety" (*ibid.*, XVII, 309).

This is the educational atmosphere from which the English colonists migrated and which was destined to give life and form to their system of instruction in the new world. So much space has been given to the situation in England, because only in this way can we understand the educational procedure in English colonial New York. And this is all the more true, since, on this latter subject, there is great paucity of material. But such data as may be found will amply justify our expectations, as I shall now proceed to show.

The religious character of education in the colony of New York after the establishment of English supremacy and under the influence of the English ideal may be seen first of all in the custom of licensing schoolmasters. The instructions to Governor Dongan, given at Windsor, May 29, 1686, contained the following regulation: "And wee doe further direct that noe Schoolmaster bee henceforth permitted to come from England and to keep school within Our Province of New York, without the license of the said Archbishop of Canterbury; and that noe other person now there or that shall come from other parts, bee admitted to keep school without your license first had" (*N.Y. Col. Doc.*, III, 372). With the substitution of the Bishop of London for the Archbishop of Canterbury this same direction is given to Governor Henry Sloughter, January 31, 1689 (*ibid.*, 688); to Governor Fletcher, March 7, 1691–92 (*ibid.*, 821); to Governor Bellemont, August 31, 1697 (*ibid.*, IV, 288); and to Governor Hunter, December 27, 1709 (*ibid.*, V, 135).

The meaning of this license is altogether unequivocal. Each of the instructions referred to above contains a clause like the following: "You shall take especial care that God Almighty be devoutly and duly served throughout your Government, the Book of Common Prayer as it is now established read each Sunday & Holy-day and the blessed Sacrament administered according to the Rites of the Church of England, You shall be carefull that the Churches already built there be well and orderly kept and more built as the Colony shall by God's blessing be improved and that besides a competent Maintenance to be assigned to the Minister of each Orthodox Church a convenient house be built at the Common Charge for each Minister and a competent proporcion of land assigned him for a Glebe and exercise of his Industry" (*ibid.*, III, 821; see also each of the references above).

It is therefore without question that the government intended to reduce the religious practices of the colony to conformity with the Church of England, and that the schoolmaster was to be a means to that end. Education was to be indoctrination.

However, this regulation fell into disuse during the administration of Governor Hunter. The last license of which there seems to be any record was issued by him to Allane Jarratt, 1712. A bill to revive the custom was introduced into the legislature, 1745, but found its quietus in the Committee of the Whole (Pratt's *Ann.*, p. 142). But in the eighteenth century, as will be shown in the next chapter, the Society for the Propagation of the Gospel took the initiative which had been exercised by the legislature, and education in the colony became dominated by the English ideal as it had not been hitherto.

Again, the religious character of education in English colonial New York finds further confirmation in the character and qualifications demanded of schoolmasters. There is not a great deal of information to be found on this topic, but the following extract from the address of the mayor, aldermen, and commonality of the city of New York to his Excellency, Governor Cornbury, relative to a teacher for the new free school of the city, will illustrate not only what kind of schoolmaster was wished, but also the point of view of leading statesmen of the time, as well as the regulation regarding license. Speaking of securing a fit person to assume charge of the school recently provided for by act of the legislature, the address proceeds as follows: "Wherefore that so good a worke may not suffer by delay nor fail of its desired end Wee the said Mayor Alderman & Commonality become most humble Supplicants to your Excellency that you would be pleased to help on the structure whose foundation you have already laid in Representing our Want of a School Master with all the difficult Circumstances thereof to the Right Reverend and no less Honourable my Lord of London and in Requesting his fatherly Care and Concern for us therein and by his Lordships means that of the Society for propagating the Gospel in foreign parts in Order to our being supplied from thence with a person of good learning pious life and vertuous Conversation of English Extract and mild temper to be our said School Master" (Pratt's *Ann.*, p. 86).

Even from these scant data it is evident that the English of colonial New York attempted to carry out in their educational policy the ideals which obtained in the home country. What these ideals were has been sufficiently illustrated in the writings of John Brinsly and Charles Hoole. And how the English of New York attempted to embody them in their educational practice has been exemplified in the gubernatorial license demanded of all teachers and in the "pious life and vertuous conversation" required of all masters of schools. The pious character of the teacher was very properly recognized as an indispensable factor in the educational process, and the schoolmaster's license was a sure lever in the hands of the church by which it might lift the educational structure to a religious and ecclesiastical basis.

CHAPTER III

EDUCATION UNDER THE AUSPICES OF THE SOCIETY FOR THE PROPAGATION OF THE GOSPEL

After the free-school act of 1702 nothing whatever, in the form of legal provision, was done for the encouragement of primary education during the remainder of the colonial period (Pratt's *Ann.*, p. 95; Hasse's Index to *Doc. of the State of N.Y.*, p. 209, under "Public Schools." This list of documents passes from 1702 to 1798 direct). The place of colonial and municipal authority was now largely superseded by the venerable Society for the Propagation of the Gospel, which, from its organization in 1701 down to the period of the Revolution, carried on, for that time, a very considerable educational work in the colony. It is the purpose of this chapter to show something of the nature and extent of this work.

Daniel J. Pratt, *Annals of Public Education in the State of New York* (pp. 111–14), has compiled a list of the Society's schoolmasters employed in the Province of New York. This list is based on the *Abstracts of Proceedings of the Society for the Propagation of the Gospel* and Bolton's *History of the Church in Westchester County* (pp. 126, 351). Besides catechists and those engaged in the teaching of Indians, there are forty-nine bona fide schoolmasters exercising their calling in seventeen towns located in seven different counties. The counties occupied were Albany, Queens, Suffolk, Montgomery, New York, Richmond, and Westchester.

As an illustration of the Society's educational work are offered the following extracts from Humphreys' *Gospel in North America:* "The Society were sensible nothing could be more convenient than the opening of Schools in this Place. The whole Island was divided into three Precincts, they appointed a schoolmaster for each. Mr. Brown taught School in the South Precinct, Mr. Dupuy in the North, and Mr. Williamson in the West. Mr. Dupuy did not keep School long; Mr. Potts succeeded him. Afterwards in the Year 1715, Mr. Taylor was appointed, and continues still teaching School; and several Accounts have been sent to the Society, that he teaches above 40 Scholars, without any Consideration but the Society's Bounty" (p. 219).

"The Society have from their first Establishment, paid Salaries to several Schoolmasters in this Government. Mr. Gilderslieve at Hempsted in Long-Island, and Mr. Taylor in Statten-Island, have been mentioned already. Mr. Huddlestone was appointed Schoolmaster in New-York City, in the Year 1709; he taught 40 poor Children for the Society's Allowance only. . . . . Mr. Glover was appointed Schoolmaster at West-Chester in the Year 1714, and afterwards Mr. Forester; he teaches between 30 and 40 Children, Catechises on Saturday and Sunday, which is certified by the Minister and chief Inhabitants of that Town. Mr. Cleator was settled Schoolmaster at Rye, in the Year 1704; he teaches about 50 Children to Read and Write, and instructs them in the Catechism. And Mr. Denton hath been lately appointed Schoolmaster at Oysterbay in Long-Island" (pp. 228, 229).

This educational work was undertaken in response to a real need in the colony. In spite of all the agitation of the subject of which the original records give evidence, there is reason to believe that in actual practice achievement was far behind promise and precept. One of the Society's missionaries, a Rev. Mr. Thomas, reporting the situation in Long Island, 1709, writes as follows: "That there was a great Want of Schools, the younger People and Children were growing up in a miserable Ignorance, for want of being taught to read; and he could not perform one Part of his Pastoral Office, Catechising, for want of a Schoolmaster to teach the Children to read. The Society appoint Mr. Gilderslieve Schoolmaster there, in the Year 1713, and allowed him a Salary to teach the poorer Children Reading, Writing, and the Rudiments of Arithmetic. The Vestry of this Parish wrote the Society a Letter on this Occasion, wherein they say: 'Without your Bounty and Charity, our poor Children would undoubtedly want all Education; our People are poor, and settled distantly from one another, and unable to board out their Children'" (Humphreys, p. 224).

The need of schools and schoolmasters in the colony is still further exemplified by the following extracts:

"As to Catechists or School-masters, the Society have, as their Ability would permit, answered many Demands upon them on that Head also, ... By continuing Mr. William Huddleston's Salary of 10 £ per Ann. for his care of the School at New York (the Maintenance of which was before uncertain and precarious); By granting 10 £ per annum each to Mr. Francis Williamson and Mr. John de Puy, for their Pains in the School-way at Staten Island, so satisfactory to the worthy Missionary there, the Reverend Mr. Aeneus Mackenzy, and so beneficial to the People as appears by an address of the Justices of Richmond County, dated June 13, 1712, and by coming to a unanimous resolution, that Three more should be forthwith allowed the Society's Pay, as Catechists or School-masters; one for the town of Hampstead in Long Island, at 10£ per Annum, upon the Request of Mr. John Thomas, Missionary there, who represents the Children thereof, for want of Letters and Education, as wild, uncultivated and unimproved, as the soil was when their Forefathers first had it" (Pratt's *Ann.*, p. 104).

Rev. Mr. Milner, sending his report from Westchester, 1726, has this to say about the school: "The school is still vacant, and deprived of a teacher, but (he) petitions the Society to continue their bounty to some worthy person who shall be chosen schoolmaster; as the school is a nursery for the church, and of great service in these parts which request is accordingly granted" (Bolton, *Hist. of Church*, etc., p. 71).

Rev. James Westmore, minister of the Parish of Rye, Westchester County, writing to the secretary of the Society, 1727, after speaking of several poor private schools, goes on to say: "But there is no public provision at all for a school in this parish, except what the Honorable Society allow Mr. Cleator, nor is there any donations or benefactions to the minister or schoolmaster, besides what I have mentioned, nor is there any library besides the Honorable Society's" (Bolton, p. 250).

"Mr. Mackenzy, the Society's Missionary in Staten Island in the Province of New York, having informed them how much they wanted School-Masters, to instruct the children of the English, Dutch, and French, in the said Island, and having recommended Mr. Adam Brown, and Mr. Benjamin Drewit, for that Purpose, the Society made choice of them both" (Pratt's *Ann.*, p. 104).

As to the nature of the schools fostered by the Society for the Propagation of the Gospel, it is necessary to remark that they were both secular and religious. They were intended to give a primary education under religious influence. In support of this proposition, the following references are cited:

"The Society sent Quantities of Paper for the Use of the School, Catechisms, and large Numbers of Common-Prayer-Books, which proved of great Benefit to the younger People. The Youth was instructed, made their Responses regularly at Church, and Divine Worship was performed with more Knowledge and Decency" (Humphreys, p. 225).

"Besides the Missionaries there has been a great Demand upon them for Catechists and School-Masters to Instruct not only the Servants and Slaves but also the Children of the Planters, especially the poorer sort, in Reading, Writing and the Principles of the Christian Religion, as Taught and Professed in the Church of England" (Pratt's *Ann.*, p. 104).

A schoolmaster is appointed at Rye, "who shall be allowed 5 £ per Annum, on a certificate that he has taught 30 such, the Bible, the Catechism, and the Use of the Liturgy" (*Abstract of Proceedings*, etc., 1712–13, p. 40; quoted in Pratt's *Ann.*, p. 105).

"From Mr. Huddleston, Schoolmaster at New York, That he teaches 50 poor children on the Society's Bounty to read and write, and instructs them in the Church Catechism, many of which are now fit for any Trade" (Pratt's *Ann.*, p. 105).

"Mr. Noxon, the schoolmaster, writes from New York, August 6, 1738, That he hath upwards of fifty poor Children, whom he teaches to read, write and cipher upon the Society's Charity; and brings to Trinity Church on Wednesdays, Fridays and Holy Days, to be catechised. He adds, there is a great want of Common Prayer-Books and Psalters" (Pratt's *Ann.*, p. 106).

The Society's abstracts for 1714 contain the following item: "To these donations the Society added two dozen prayer books for Mr. Huddleston, with the old version of the singing, and as many of Lewis' Church catechism, for exercise in his school or on mornings of the Lord's days, (when not only his own scholars, but several of the young people of the town, of both sexes, came willingly to be informed) one dozen bibles with the common prayer and the new version of psalms, twenty-five psalters, and fifty-one primers, all which he requested as contributing mightily, to the spreading the good work he has in hand, having taught besides British children, six hundred Dutch and French, to read and write English" (Bolton, *Hist. of the Church*, etc., p. 204).

From the evidence already given there can be no question that the Society's schools taught reading, writing, and ciphering, but that they were distinctly religious and ecclesiastical in aim is still further authenticated by the following extract from the instructions for schoolmasters employed by the Society:

"I. That they well consider the End for which they are employed by the Society, viz. The instructing and disposing Children to believe and live as Christians.

"II. In order to this End, that they teach them to read truly and distinctly, that they may be capable of reading the Holy Scriptures, and other pious and useful Books, for informing their Understandings and regulating their manners.

"III. That they instruct them thoroughly in the Church-Catechism; teach them first to read it distinctly and exactly, then to learn it perfectly by Heart; endeavoring to make them understand the Sense and

Meaning of it, by the Help of such Expositions, as the Society shall send over.

"IV. That they teach them to Write a plain and legible Hand, in order to the fitting them for useful Employments; with as much Arithmetic, as shall be necessary to the same purpose.

. . . .

"VI. That they daily use, Morning and Evening, the Prayers composed for their Use in this Collection with their Scholars in the School, and teach them the Prayers and Graces composed for their Use at Home.

"VII. That they oblige their Scholars to be constant at Church on the Lord's-Day Morning and Afternoon, and at all other Times of Publick Worship; that they cause them to carry their Bibles and Prayer Books with them, instructing them how to use them there, and how to demean themselves in the several Parts of Worship; that they be there present with them, taking Care of their reverent and decent Behavior, and examine them afterwards as to what they have heard and learned" (Pratt's *Ann.*, p. 109).

The facts set forth in this chapter go to show the extent and nature of the educational work carried on in the Province of New York by the Society for the Propagation of the Gospel. Since colonial and municipal interest had waned, the Society came in to supply a real educational need. There was no other educational agency in the colony at that time so conspicuous in its activities for the public good. Yet, as we have seen, the ultimate purpose of the Society for the Propagation of the Gospel was other than educational, and reading and writing were taught the children merely as a gateway to the Bible and Catechism and the Prayer-Book. The end sought was religious education.

CHAPTER IV

EDUCATIONAL MOVEMENTS OF THE EARLY NINETEENTH CENTURY

Hasse enumerates the following church schools operative in the city of New York for the greater part of the first quarter of the nineteenth century, and some of them continuing still longer: Christ Church, Bethel Baptist Church, Scotch Presbyterian Church, First Presbyterian Church, German Lutheran Church, Methodist Episcopal Church, St. Michael's Church, First Baptist Church, Episcopal Charity School, Reformed Dutch, St. Peter's Church Free School, St. Patrick's Cathedral Free School (Index to *Doc. of State of N.Y.*, under "Private and Parochial Schools"). How widely these schools were established throughout the state it is perhaps now impossible to tell, but there is no reason to suppose that the city of New York enjoyed a monopoly of this good work. These church schools were for the education of the poor and were, as a matter of course, religious in aim and method.

In 1805 a corporation was formed in the city of New York, known at first as the Free School Society, afterward as the Public School Society. Its original object was the education of the children of the poor who did not belong to, or were not provided for by, any religious denomination. But feeling that this restriction unnecessarily limited their sphere of usefulness, this society in 1808, received authority from the legislature to educate all children who were proper objects of gratuitous instruction. The Free School Society of the city of New York was one of the most conspicuous educational agencies of the state until in the year 1853 it was merged into the general system of common instruction (Ann. Reports and Manuscript Records in custody of N.Y. Historical Society Library).

The early records of this Society clearly indicate its position on the question of religious instruction in the schools of the people. Instruction was to be religious but not sectarian. The following extracts from the Society's address to the public, 1805, will illustrate this point:

"While the various religious and benevolent societies in this city, with a spirit of charity and zeal which the precepts and example of the Divine Author of our religion could alone inspire, amply provide for the education of such poor children as belong to their respective associations, there still remains a large number living in total neglect of religious and moral instruction, and unacquainted with the common rudiments of learning, essentially requisite for the due management of the ordinary business of life" (Bourne, *History of the Public School Society*, p. 6).

"It is proposed, also, to establish, on the first day of the week, a school, called a Sunday School, more particularly for such children as, from peculiar circumstances, are unable to attend on the other days of the week. In this, as in the Common School, it will be a primary object, without observing the peculiar forms of any religious Society, to inculcate the sublime truths of religion and morality contained in the Holy Scriptures" (Bourne, p. 7).

The attitude of the Society is still further and fully illustrated by the following extracts from its annual reports:

"While the Trustees have been thus engaged in communicating, to the understandings of the children, the elements of useful knowledge, they have not been unmindful of the importance of imbuing their minds also with a sense of moral and religious obligation.

"The afternoon of every Tuesday, or third day of the week, has been set apart for this purpose; and the children have been instructed in the catechisms of the churches to which they respectively belong. This pious office is performed by an association of highly respectable females, who are in profession with the different religious denominations in the city. The number of children, educated in the peculiar tenets of each religious community, is, at the present, as follows: Presbyterians 271, Episcopalians 186, Methodists 172, Baptists 119, Dutch Church 41, Roman Catholic 9" (*Ninth Annual Report*, 1814, not paged).

"The office of communicating religious instruction to the children, by teaching them the Catechisms of their respective Churches, is still performed by the Association of benevolent females, who are zealously engaged in it" (*Tenth Annual Report*, 1815).

"The children continue to receive the advantages of religious instruction, communicated to them from the catechisms used in the respective churches to which they belong, in the manner mentioned in the report of last year" (*Eleventh Annual Report*, 1816).

Speaking of the Society's work, the report says: "It has happily brought the means of education within the reach of all classes of people; and, gradually diffusing among them the light of knowledge and of religion, must have a powerful tendency to ameliorate the condition of Society and to advance the best interests of our country" (*Twelfth Annual Report*, 1817).

"With gratitude we acknowledge a donation of 61 Bibles, and 50 Testaments from the New-York Auxiliary Bible Society, and of 25

Bibles, from the New-York Bible Society" (*Fourteenth Annual Report*, 1819).

"No new books for the instruction of children in the Free-Schools, have been introduced during the past year. The Scripture lessons continue to be used with all the advantages contemplated at the time of their adoption, and it affords satisfaction to find a book so useful, becoming popular over the continent of Europe, and to hear of its being introduced in South America" (*Eighteenth Annual Report*, 1823).

From the extracts cited above it appears evident that the Free School Society was deeply interested in the religious instruction of the children, although from the beginning it recognized the importance of avoiding sectarian differences.

The religious motive in the founding of common schools is clearly evidenced by the public utterances of prominent statesmen of the time. In his message to the legislature, 1787, Governor Clinton said in part: "Neglect of the education of youth is one of the evils consequent upon war. Perhaps there is scarce anything more worthy your attention than the revival and encouragement of seminaries of learning; and nothing by which we can more satisfactorily express our gratitude to the Supreme Being for his past favors—since piety and virtue are generally the offspring of an enlightened understanding" (quoted by Randall, *History of the Common School System of the State of N.Y.*, p. 8).

Governor Tompkins in his legislative message, 1810, declared his conviction as follows: "I cannot omit this occasion of inviting your attention to the means of instruction for the rising generation. To enable them to perceive and duly to estimate their rights; to inculcate correct principles and habits of morality and religion; and to render them useful citizens, a competent provision for their education is all-essential" (Randall, p. 15).

In 1811, Governor Tompkins, by act of legislature, appointed a commission of five to report a plan for the establishment and organization of common schools. This report was presented to the legislature, February 17, 1812, and embodied the main features of the common-school system up to 1840. The following extracts will show the remarkable influence of the religious motive:

"To rescue man from that state of degradation to which he is doomed, unless redeemed by education; to unfold his physical, intellectual, and moral powers; and fit him for those high destinies which his Creator has prepared for him, cannot fail to excite the most ardent sensibility of the philosopher and the philanthropist."

After pointing out relation of education to good morals and free government, the report proceeds as follows: "The Commissioners think it unnecessary to represent in a stronger point of view the importance and absolute necessity of education, as connected either with the cause of religion and morality, or with the prosperity and existence of our political institutions."

This education is to be provided by the establishment of common schools spread throughout the state. "This appears to be the best plan that can be devised to disseminate religion, morality, and learning throughout a whole country."

As to what should be taught in these schools the report says: "Reading, writing, arithmetic, and the principles of morality are essential to every person, however humble his situation in life. Without the first, it is impossible to receive those lessons of morality which are inculcated in the writings of the learned and pious; nor is it possible to become acquainted with our political constitutions and laws, nor to decide those great political questions which ultimately are referred to the intelligence of the people. Writing and arithmetic are indispensable in the management of one's private affairs, and to facilitate one's commerce with the world. Morality and religion are the foundation of all that is truly great and good; and are, consequently, of primary importance."

The commission is solicitous as to the introduction of proper books into the contemplated schools. "Much good is to be derived from a judicious selection of books, calculated to enlighten the understanding not only, but to improve the heart. And as it is of incalculable consequence to guard the young and tender mind from receiving fallacious impressions, the Commissioners cannot omit mentioning this subject as a part of the weighty trust reposed in them. Connected with the introduction of suitable books, the Commissioners take the liberty of suggesting that some observation and advice touching the reading of the Bible in the schools might be salutary. In order to render the sacred volume productive of the greatest advantage, it should be held in a very different light from that of a common school book. It should be regarded as a book intended for literary improvement, not merely, but as inculcating great and indispensable moral truths also. With these impressions the Commissioners are induced to recommend the practice introduced into the New York Free Schools, of having select chapters read at the opening of the school in the morning, and the like at the close in the afternoon. This is deemed the best mode of preserving the religious regard which is due to the sacred writings."

"And the Commissioners cannot but hope that that Being who rules the universe in justice and in mercy, who rewards virtue and punishes vice, will most graciously deign to smile benignly on the humble efforts of a people in a cause purely His own; and that He will manifest His pleasure in the lasting prosperity of our country" (entire document reproduced in Randall, pp. 17–23).

A bill embodying this report was passed by the legislature 1812 and, as stated above, remained in force till about 1840. As the report of a legislative commission it is evidence of the first order in support of the contention that the common schools were founded, in part at least, from a religious motive, and that religious instruction was to form a part of their curriculum.

CHAPTER V

ELEMENTARY-SCHOOL BOOKS OF THE EIGHTEENTH CENTURY

We have already seen in the preceding chapters the use of religious material in the schools in the form of psalters and catechisms, as well as in the reading of the Bible itself. It is the purpose of the present chapter to take a step farther in advance, and show the religious character of the more important school books of the colonial period and the early days of the republic.

One of the best authorities on this subject (Johnson, *Old-Time Schools and School-Books*, p. 185) gives the following very interesting summary: "John Locke, in 1690, said of elementary education in England, 'The method is to adhere to the ordinary road of the Horn-book, Primer, Psalter, Testament, and Bible; these are the only books used to engage the liking of children and tempt them to read.' 'The ordinary road' was the same here. There were three reading classes in the schools—'The Psalter Class' for beginners, next 'The Testament Class,' and thirdly 'The Bible Class,' which went through about two chapters at each school session and was expected to spell the words in the portions read. For a long time spelling-books were lacking, and they did not become common much before 1750; but after that time for fully three-quarters of a century the spelling-book was almost the sole resource of the school children for elementary instruction. Advanced readers were in the market in the early years of the republic, but readers for the beginners seem to have been thought unnecessary. Thus the spellers of the forefathers did double duty as spelling-books and primers, and were a much more important institution than they have ever been since."

Disregarding, as not calling for further consideration, psalters, Testaments, and Bibles, our present study will be confined to hornbooks, primers, spelling-books, and readers. The hornbook consisted of a small sheet of paper pasted on a board and covered with transparent horn as a protection for the printing underneath. It had its beginnings in the Middle Ages and persisted far down in the eighteenth century. It was advertised in a Philadelphia newspaper so late as 1770 (*Pennsylvania Gazette*). The alphabet, the Lord's Prayer, some verses of Scripture or moral precepts, and some stanzas of poetry composed its course of study (Tuer, *History of the Horn-Book*).

The hornbook was widely used in this country as well as abroad. The chief evidence of this fact is the advertisements of booksellers in the newspapers of such cities as Boston, New York, and Philadelphia. The *New York Gazette* of November 6, 1738 advertises hornbooks for sale. The *New York Gazette Revived in the Weekly Post-Boy* has a similar advertisement on June 27, 1748; also in the issue of July 25, 1748; also in 1753.

An interesting advertisement is found in the *New York Weekly Post-Boy* of August 19, 1745: "John Hinsliew, Book seller advertises Past Board Books to answer the End of Hornbooks for little children." The fact that the "Book seller" wishes the people to know that he has something that will serve as a satisfactory substitute for hornbooks seems good evidence to the effect that the latter were in use at that time, or had been, not a great while before.

The primer is an expanded hornbook, and for its origin goes back to the Romish Abecedariums of the fifteenth century. It figured largely in the English Reformation and was very early brought to the American Colonies (Ford, *New England Primer*, pp. 1–12). Primers were advertised in the New York papers certainly as early as 1738 (*New York Gazette*, November 6, 1738). Similar advertisements are found in the *New York Weekly Post-Boy*, December 24, 1744, December 2, 1745; the *New York Mercury*, September 30, 1754, October 14, 1754, June 7, 1756, July 18, 1757. There were also the *New York Primer* published 1747 (*New York Evening Post*, September 7, 1747), *Church of England Primer* (*New York Gazette Revived in the Weekly Post-Boy*, June 27, 1748), and, in Pennsylvania, at least, there were Quaker and Presbyterian Primers (*Pennsylvania Gazette*, January 6, 1742).

But the queen of them all was the *New England Primer*. It was first published in Boston, between 1687 and 1690, by Benjamin Harris. It seems to have been a success from the beginning, as a second and enlarged edition was printed in 1691 (Ford, p. 16). Its circulation was enormous. Paul Leicester Ford, in his scholarly work on the subject (p. 19), thus describes its great popularity. "For one hundred years this Primer was *the* school-book of the dissenters of America, and for another hundred, it was frequently reprinted. In the unfavorable locality (in a sectarian sense) of Philadelphia, the accounts of Benjamin Franklin and David Hall show that between 1749 and 1766, or a period of seventeen years, that firm sold thirty-seven thousand, one hundred copies. Livermore stated in 1849 that within the last dozen years '100,000 copies of modern editions . . . . have been circulated.' An over-conservative claim for it is to estimate an annual average sale of twenty thousand copies during a period of one hundred and fifty years, or total sales of three million copies."

But our chief concern is in the distribution of the Primer in the Province of New York. And while there is not the wealth of evidence that some might wish, there is perhaps no student of the subject who does not feel morally certain of the wide use of the *New England Primer* in the New York of the eighteenth century. Nor are we left to conjecture. Evans' *American Bibliography* (III, No. 6726) contains the following interesting announcement:

"THE NEW ENGLAND PRIMRE (*sic*) IMPROVED, FOR THE MORE EASY ATTAINING THE TRUE READING OF ENGLISH. TO WHICH IS ADDED, THE ASSEMBLY OF DIVINES CATECHISM.

"New York: Printed and sold by James Parker, in Beaver-Street, 1750."

This is the earliest known date at which the *New England Primer* was printed in New York City, but it was advertised for sale as early as 1748, July 25, in the *New York Gazette:* "Writing Books for School-Boys, New England Primers; Church of England Primers; Horn-Books." Also the advertisements of primers in general, referred to above, are in point here. It is an interesting fact that by far the larger number of these advertisements do not designate any particular primer. Their names were well known. Designation was therefore unnecessary. But the *New England Primer* was the most notable of them all, and, without doubt, was in every advertiser's collection. Now the fact that the *New England Primer* was published and advertised by booksellers in New York is conclusive evidence of its use in that section of the country.

In the course of its long and popular career the *New England Primer* suffered many minor alterations at the hands of printers and publishers, yet through all retained unmistakable marks of its identity. Despite incidental changes, it usually contained the alphabet, easy syllables for children, sentences of moral and religious instruction, the rhymed alphabet, or short poems illustrating each letter, Lord's Prayer, Creed, and Catechism. Except the alphabet and words for spelling, it was exclusively a religious book, and its widespread use throughout the eighteenth century warrants a more detailed statement of its contents (see Ford's Introduction).

I have in hand a reprint of the edition of 1777. Immediately after the title-page the reader comes to two prayers: "The young Infant's or Child's morning prayer"; "The Infant's or young Child's Evening Prayer," both by Dr. Watts. These prayers are followed by six pages of letters, syllables, and spelling. Then comes the "rhymed alphabet." Each letter is illustrated by a little cut and a rhymed couplet, such as the following:

A. "In Adam's Fall
We sinned all."

B. "Heaven to find,
The Bible Mind."

Every couplet of the twenty-four is religious in its tone, and nearly every one a reference to the Bible. This, however, was not the case in editions prior to 1740 (Ford, p. 46). Next follows a series of questions with such answers as Adam, Eve, Noah, Job, Jesus Christ, Son of God, etc. The alphabet of lessons fills the next two pages, each one of which is a quotation from the Bible. Now come the Lord's Prayer, the creed, Dr. Watts's Cradle Hymn, and verses for children. These last cover seven pages and start off with the following:

"Though I am young a little one,
If I can speak and go alone,
Then I must learn to know the Lord,
And learn to read his holy word.
'Tis time to seek to God and pray
For what I want for every day:
I have a precious soul to save,
And I a mortal body have,
Tho' I am young yet I may die,
And hasten to eternity:
There is a dreadful fiery hell,
Where wicked ones must always dwell:
There is a heaven full of joy,
Where godly ones must always stay:
To one of these my soul must fly,
As in a moment when I die."

After ten more pages of varied religious material comes "The Shorter Catechism, Agreed upon by the Reverend Assembly of Divines at Westminster." This in turn is followed by "Spiritual Milk For American Babes, Drawn out of the Breasts of both Testaments for their Souls Nourishment. By John Cotton." After this "Spiritual Milk" comes "A Dialogue between Christ, Youth, and the Devil." This array of religious and theological pabulum reaches a fitting conclusion with advice to children by the Reverend and Venerable Nathaniel Clap, of Newport, Rhode Island: "Good children should remember daily, God their Creator, Redeemer, and Sanctifier; to believe in, love and serve him; their parents to obey them in the Lord; their bible and catechism; their baptism; the Lord's day; the Lord's death and resurrection; their own death and resurrection; and the day of judgment, when all that are not fit for heaven must be sent to hell. And they should pray to God in the name of Christ, for saving grace."

Coote's *English School-Master* was one of the earliest so-called spelling-books, published first in 1590. It contained about seventy-two pages, of which eighteen were given to a "Short Catechism, necessary observations of a Christian, prayers, and psalms" (Littlefield, *Early Schools & School-Books of New England*, p. 120). According to the author just quoted (p. 119) this book was extensively used in the New England schools of the seventeenth century. While positive evidence is lacking, there seems no reason to doubt its use in New York as well.

About a century later than Coote's *School-Master*, 1708, was published an interesting textbook for schools, called *The History of Genesis.* It was composed of short narratives from the first book of the Bible. Its title-page reads in part as follows: "The History of Genesis. Being an Account of the Holy Lives and Actions of the Patriarchs; explained with Pious and Edifying Explications, and illustrated with near Forty Figures. Fitted for the Use of Schools, and recommended to Teachers of Children, as a Book very proper for the learning them to read English, and instructing them in the right understanding of these Divine Histories" (Johnson, p. 45).

Neither of the two books named in the paragraphs above was a speller in the strict sense of the word. They are mentioned here because they were introductory to that class of school books, and show as well as any the religious character of the instruction, which was characteristic of the time.

The speller that was most widely used in the eighteenth century was Dilworth's *A New Guide to the English Tongue.* This was published in 1740, and for about fifty years enjoyed unrivaled popularity. That it found a place in the schools of New York is placed beyond the peradventure of doubt. The following newspaper advertisements of booksellers are quite conclusive: *New York Mercury*, June 27, 1748, July 22, 1754, November 8, 1762, and *New York Gazette and Weekly Mercury*, June 25, 1770. One of these advertisements says: "Dilworth's Spelling Book: very cheap by the dozen." Another reads: "Dilworth's Spelling-Book by the Wholesale." No doubt there are numerous advertisements which have not come to notice, but those referred to above cover a period of twenty-two years and can have no explanation apart from a very general demand for the book in question.

The conviction that Dilworth's *Speller* was very widely used in the Province of New York, and that it is typical of the school books of the period calls for some account of its contents. As indicating the general character of the book and the educational spirit of the times, the following extracts from the preface will be suggestive:

"It has been a general and true Observation, that with the Reformation of these Realms, Ignorance has gradually vanished and the increase of Learning amongst us, who take the Word of God for a Lantern to our Feet, and a Light to our Paths. Thus,

"They who grop'd their Way to Virtue and Knowledge in the Days of Darkness and implicit Zeal, were taught little more than to mumble over a few Prayers by Heart, and never called upon to read, much less permitted to enquire into the Truth of what they professed. But

"Since the Sunshine of the Gospel of Jesus Christ has risen amongst us; since we are loosed from the Bands of Ignorance and Superstition; since every Protestant believes it to be his Duty to promote Christian Knowledge; certainly it will be confessed, that all Improvements in Learning ought to be encouraged; and consequently that they deserve our particular Regard, who study to make the first Steps therefore firm and easy. For human Prudence teacheth, That a good Beginning is the most reasonable Prospect of a good Ending. Therefore,

"As we boast of greater Advantages than our Forefathers, let us take care, lest we frustrate the great Work begun amongst us, by negligent Prosecution of our Duty: For I would have you well assured, that it is as bad to learn the first Rudiments of Literature under wrong and depraved Habits, as not to learn them at all. For, the Man seldom clears himself of these ill Faculties, which are contracted in his tender Age: So, says Solomon, Train up a Child in the Way he should go, and when he is old he will not depart from it" (p. iv).

The first part of the book covers seventy-six pages. The plan of instruction is to give several pages of letters and syllables, followed by short reading lessons of two or three pages. Here is a sample page of the reading:

"Shew me the right Way, O Lord, and guide me in it.
"O think not on my past Sins; but think on me, O Lord, for my good.
"All the Paths of the Lord are True to such as keep his Laws.
"He that doth love the Lord shall dwell at Ease; and his Seed shall have the Land."

"Put thy Trust in God, and he will help thee.
"It is a good Thing to give Thanks, and to call on the Name of the Lord.
"Let us sing Psalms to the Lord our God.
"When thou shalt make a Vow to the Lord thy God, thou shalt not be slack to pay it."

"That which is gone out of thy Lips, thou shalt keep: And if a Man vow to the Lord, he shall keep his Oath.
"Let us stand fast. Let us strive to be good.
"Charge them that are Rich in this World, that they do good, and be glad to give" (p. 19).

The second and third parts of the book are taken up with a table of useful words and a study of grammatical construction. Part IV is "An useful Collection of Sentences in Prose and Verse, Divine, Moral, and Historical." Many of these "verses" are much like the following: "Repentance, though it is not to be rested in as any Satisfaction for Sin, or any Cause of the Pardon thereof, which is the Act of God's free Grace in Christ; yet it is of such Necessity to all Sinners, that none may expect Pardon without it" (p. 130).

Part V consists wholly of "Forms of Prayer for Children, on several Occasions." The purpose of these prayers, according to the preface, is to teach the pupils "that all their Dependence is on God, by whom we live, and move, and have our Being" (p. ix; all references to ed. of 1773).

The year 1783 witnessed the first spelling-book by an American author. It bore the ponderous title of *The First Part of a Grammatical Institute of the English Language*, by Noah Webster. This book superseded Dilworth's *Speller* and for a time outrivaled all competitors. Its circulation was so extensive that the author, during the twenty years he was compiling his famous dictionary, was able handsomely to support himself and family from the proceeds of its sale, although his premium was less than one cent per copy.

From the point of view of religious material, Webster's *Speller* stands in striking contrast with Dilworth's. The former, however, while predominantly moral, was not destitute of religious instruction. The first 43 pages were devoted wholly to spelling. At this point reading lessons are interspersed. The following is an example of its religious tone:

"No man may put off the law of God;
My joy is in his law all the day.
O may I not go in the way of sin!
Let me not go in the way of ill men" (Johnson, p. 176).

The last twelve pages of the book are devoted to "A Moral Catechism." The following question and answer may be considered religious as well as moral:

"Q. Is pride commendable?

"A. By no means. A modest, self-approving opinion of our own good deeds is very right—it is natural—it is agreeable, and a spur to good actions. But we should not suffer our hearts to be blown up with pride; for pride brings upon us the ill-will of mankind, and displeasure of our Maker" (Johnson, p. 180).

Speaking of the changes in the revised edition of 1829, Clifton Johnson says: "The Moral Catechism was omitted, and so were the scattered religious and ethical lessons" (p. 181).

As indicating the scarcity of elementary readers during the first years of the nineteenth century, also as evidence of the wide use at that time of the Testament as a reading-book, I reproduce a part of the preface to Leavitt's *Easy Lessons in Reading*, New Hampshire, 1823: "The compiler has been excited to the present undertaking by representations that there is no reading book to be found at the book stores, suitable for young children, to be used intermediately, between the Spelling-Book and the English or American Reader. The Testament is much used for this purpose; and on many accounts, it is admirably adapted for a reading book in schools. But it is respectfully submitted to the experience of judicious teachers, whether the peculiar structure of scripture language is not calculated to create a tone? I am persuaded it would be better to place a book in the hands of learners, written in a more familiar style" (quoted in Johnson, p. 240).

The Franklin Primer had been published in 1802. It was intended as a substitute for the *New England Primer*, "which has of late become almost obsolete." The little volume contained "a variety of tables, moral lessons and sentences, a concise history of the World, appropriate Hymns, and Dr. Watts and the Assembly of Divines' Catechisms" (Johnson, p. 234).

In 1808, *The Child's Instructor* was published at Philadelphia. The following paragraphs will indicate its religious tone:

"Good boys and girls go to church. Do you go to church? Billy went to church, and so did Betsey. The church is the house of God; and God loves little children when they go to church."

"When you go to church you must sit still, and hear what the preacher tells you; he tells you to be good children and love your parents, and then God will bless you."

"Do you know who makes it rain? I will tell you: God makes it rain. You see that dark cloud rising in the west? That cloud will bring thunder and lightning and rain. You need not be afraid; God makes it thunder; and he will not let it hurt you if you are good" (Johnson, p. 237).

These little books may or may not have been used in New York State. They are mentioned here to indicate the spirit of the times, and as illustrative of the school books of the period.

Two very popular Advanced Readers were published by Caleb Bingham, Boston: *The American Preceptor*, 1794, and *The Columbia Orator*, 1797. In the course of time *The Columbia Orator* displaced the Bible in the schools, which was then read as a devotional exercise at the opening of the morning, and close of the afternoon, session (Littlefield, p. 156).

Clifton Johnson thus describes the character of these readers: "Most of the early reading books drew their material largely from British sources, and American contributions were for a long time mainly from the speeches of the Revolutionary orators. Typical subjects were: Frailty of Life, Benevolence of the Deity, Popery, Rules for Moderating Our Anger, Reflections on Sun Set, Character of a Truly Polite Man, The Child Trained Up for the Gallows. These and the rest of their kind were all 'extracted from the books of the most correct and elegant writers.' The books were also pretty sure to contain selections from the Bible, and some had parts of sermons. Indeed, nearly all the matter was of a serious, moral, or religious character" (p. 277).

About 1790 Noah Webster published a reader, called *The Little Reader's Assistant.* The title-page of a 1791 edition reads in part as follows:

"I. A number of Stories, mostly taken from the history of America, and adorned with Cuts.

"II. Rudiments of English Grammar.

"III. A Federal Catechism, being a short and easy explanation of the Constitution of the United States.

"IV. General Principles of Government and Commerce.

"V. The Farmer's Catechizm, containing plain rules of husbandry" (Johnson, p. 269).

This statement of the contents of *The Little Reader's Assistant* offers not the slightest suggestion of religious material. And the final part, "The Farmer's Catechizm," would perhaps be the last place where we should expect to find it. The following question and answer then will be somewhat of a surprise:

"Q. Why is farming the most innocent employment?

"A. Because farmers have fewer temptations to be wicked than other men. They live much by themselves, so that they do not see so many bad examples as men in cities do. They have but little dealings with others, so that they have fewer opportunities to cheat than other classes of men. Besides, the flocks and herds which surround the farmer, the frolicks of the harmless lambs, the songs of the cheerful birds, and the face of nature's works, all present to the husbandman examples of innocence, duty, simplicity and order, which ought to impress good sentiments on the mind and lead the heart to God" (quoted in Johnson, p. 276).

Recollections of Fifty Years Since (Astor Library, New York), by Ezekiel Bacon, constitutes an interesting side light on this curriculum of study. Ezekiel Bacon was born in Boston, Massachusetts, in 1776. He was graduated from Yale College, 1794, and shortly afterward entered the legal profession. In 1816 he went to Utica, New York, where he remained a resident until his death in 1870. He represented his adopted state in the legislature, became judge of the Court of Common Pleas, and was member of the state constitutional convention of 1821. So, while he was a New Englander by birth and training, he was thoroughly identified with the state of his adoption, and acquainted with its educational history. The address in question was delivered at Utica, 1843, to the Young Men's Association of the city (Appleton's *Cyclopaedia of American Biography*). Recollections of fifty years since that date take the reader back to the close of the previous century. Speaking of the common schools, Mr. Bacon says:

"The time is well recollected (for the speaker was one of the subjects of their stinted instructions) when little beyond Dillworth's Spelling Book, the New England Primer, teaching by a double process the first letter of the alphabet, and the first doctrine of the creed, through the instrumentality of the first poetical distich that the young minstrels of future times were taught to jingle together—

'In Adam's fall
We sinned all,'

when these recondite volumes, together with the Psalter, and in process of time and intellectual juvenile development, the other portions of the Bible, constituted about the whole of the science of common school reading then taught."

To this was added writing and a meager amount of arithmetic.

This, he says, was the general range and grade of what was esteemed to be a good country common-school education fifty years since.

As to the intellectual education of the female portion of the population during the last century, the address continues: "How little more have we to say than that they learned at their transient country schools, taught by some smart spinster, to read passably in the Bible; to repeat there, and on Saturday or Sunday evenings at home, the Shorter Catechism, which, if they fully understood when they had got through it, they certainly had sharper intellects than had some of their teachers; to get by heart Watt's Spiritual Songs; scrawl a miserable hand writing; and if deemed apt proficients and ambitious of teaching others in their turn, to dig out their way through the first four rules of Arithmetic."

The books so briefly described in this chapter are intended to illustrate the spirit that brooded over elementary education during the period under consideration. Some of them may not have been used in New York, but the books used in that province could not have been essentially different. They contained an amount of religious material, and displayed a religious spirit and motive that strike astonishment to the investigator of the present day. The elementary-school books of the eighteenth century therefore make an important contribution to our subject. They reinforce the arguments and make strong the position advocated in the chapters gone before, that religious education was incorporated in the schools of the State and City of New York from the days of the first settlement down through the early decades of the republic.

PART II

RELIGIOUS INSTRUCTION EXCLUDED FROM THE SCHOOLS

CHAPTER VI

THE RISING CONSCIOUSNESS OF SECTARIANISM IN EDUCATION

We have seen how, from the first settlement of the Province of New York, public education was carried on in the atmosphere of religion, being actuated by the religious motive, and constituted so largely of religious material. We have also seen the spirit and purpose of religion wrought into the foundations of the common-school system of the state. But in the closing years of the first quarter of the nineteenth century conditions arose which made sectarian education a problem in the consciousness of the people, and which were destined to have far-reaching results on the final solution of the question. It is the purpose of the present chapter to show how the problem arose in the consciousness of the people and what was the first verdict of public opinion in relation to the subject.

In 1813 the legislature passed a law (for basis of historical statement following see *Annual Report of Free School Society*, 1824) specifying the participants of the school fund apportioned to the City of New York. The organizations named were the Free School Society, the Orphan Asylum Society, the Economical School Society, the African Free School, and "such incorporated religious societies in said city, as now support or hereafter shall establish Charity Schools within the said city, who may apply for the same" (*Laws of New York*, 36th session, p. 38). Soon after the passage of this law, encouraged by its proffer to "incorporated religious societies," a number of religious bodies in the city established schools and were admitted to participation in the fund. By the sixth section of the law the several societies therein named participants in the fund were prohibited from using any portion of their respective shares for any purpose except the payment of teachers.

In 1817 the legislature passed an act allowing the Free School Society the privilege of using what surplus there might be left, after the payment of teachers, to the erection of school buildings, the education of schoolmasters on the Lancasterian plan, and to all needful purposes of common-school education. This special privilege was granted the Free School Society because it had been organized for the sole purpose of educating the poor, and because its property must ever be devoted to this object. The fact that the Society had a surplus, after the payment of teachers, was due to the economy of the Lancasterian system of instruction.

In 1820 Bethel Baptist Church opened a school in the basement of its building, in Delancey Street, for the reception of poor children of all denominations. The following year they drew from the school fund on basis of the law of 1813. And in 1822 the trustees of the said church obtained from the legislature the passage of a law allowing them the same privilege, which, five years before, had been granted the Free School Society. Alone among all the religious societies, this church now had the right to use its surplus for the erection of new buildings, education of teachers, etc.

The passage of this law immediately alarmed the trustees of the Free School Society, and also a number of religious societies in the city. It was believed that the door had been opened wide for the perversion of the school fund, that the church receiving the privilege above mentioned would be strongly induced to employ poor teachers at a cheap rate in order that there might be a surplus for the erection of buildings, and that the buildings thus erected would belong to the church and not to the public and would probably be devoted to other purposes than those of the education of poor children. On account of this alarm memorials from the Free School Society, from trustees of a number of church schools, and from the corporation of the city were presented to the legislature in 1823, praying the repeal of that section of the law which granted special privilege to Bethel Baptist Church.

The educational project of Bethel Church was working injury to the Free School Society. They were drawing scholars from the Society's schools and so diminishing its share of the school fund, which was apportioned to each school according to the number of scholars taught. The Bethel schools also drew large amounts of the fund appropriated to the city, thus leaving a smaller balance to be divided among other institutions of the city. Notwithstanding this, the free schools would have continued to be useful and the Society would not have pressed its opposition to the Bethel schools, but for the fact that other denominations began to manifest a disposition to follow the example of the Bethel Church, "to the extent of enlarging their schools, so as to receive for instruction poor children generally, without restricting themselves as heretofore, to those of their own particular congregations. A school of this discription has been opened in Grace Church, under the pastoral care of Rev. Mr. Wainwright; another for the education of female children, by the Congregational Church in Chamber-street; and a third will soon be opened by the Dutch Church, in the large rooms in Harmony Hall, at the corner of William, in Duane-street" (*Nineteenth Annual Report of the Free School Society*).

The Free School Society was now no longer satisfied with the repeal of the special privilege granted to the Bethel Baptist Church, but began to advocate a law restricting all church schools to the poor children connected with their respective congregations. At this time also the Society began to advocate the view that the school fund was purely of a civil character and for a civil purpose, and that it should never go into the hands of an ecclesiastical body or religious society. This position was unanimously indorsed by the city corporation, mayor, and aldermen, and also by a number of clergymen and boards of trustees of religious societies in the city (for the basis of the historical statement given thus far, see *Annual Report of the Free School Society*, April 30, 1824).

As the result of the activity of the Free School Society the legislature passed a law, November 19, 1824 (*Laws of New York*, p. 338, sec. IV), conferring upon the Common Council of the City of New York the right to name the schools which should be allowed to participate in the school fund. The scenes of conflict were thus transferred from Albany to the Council Chamber of the city corporation.

The church schools had made a hard fight. Their representatives at Albany had exhausted every argument to ward off the repeal of the privileges which had been granted them (Bourne, *History of Public School Society*, p. 73). They were equally insistent in presenting their claims to the Common Council, when the matter was brought before that body in 1825. Memorials were presented to the Council from the trustees of the charity schools attached to the Reformed Protestant Dutch Church, the First Protestant Episcopal Charity School, the trustees of the Methodist Episcopal Church, and the trustees of St. Patrick's Cathedral and St. Peter's Church. (These memorials may be found in *Archives of New York City-Hall*, Collection of April 11, 1825.) There was considerable feeling against the Free School Society, as is shown by the following extract from the memorial of the Reformed Protestant Dutch Church:

"That from a law passed by the Legislature of this state at their last extra session, your Memorialists perceive that your honorable Board have the power to designate the institutions or schools, which shall be entitled to receive any portion of the Common School Fund, and to prescribe the limitations and restrictions under which it shall be received.

"From other unquestionable sources, your Memorialists have also learnt, that strenuous and indefatigable efforts have been, and still are making, in a certain quarter, under the pleasing, though fallacious mask of unlimited philanthropy, to monopolize to themselves the exclusive right of educating the poor. To subserve this end they have not been content to exhibit to the public view what has been and what might be the extent of their own labors in the field of gratuitous education—they have attempted to prostrate the claims of their competitors, by condescending indiscriminately to brand them with odious epithets, and to undervalue their usefulness, by representations not consistent with a strict narrative of truth."

The memorials of the trustees of the First Protestant Episcopal Charity School is not so bitter in its insinuations, but just as strong in its advocacy of what it considers to be the rights of the people for whom it speaks. They wish to receive from the public fund according to the statute of 1813, and should any deviation from this plan be sanctioned, they have, they think, special claim for consideration. Their school dates back to 1711, being, they think, the first establishment for gratuitous instruction in the city. It has extended useful education to multitudes of poor children connected with the parish of Trinity Church. They had been admitted to participation in the public fund at the passage of the law in 1813, and this assistance had enabled them to double their accommodations. They believe the portion of the public fund fallen to them has been "faithfully, efficiently, and exclusively applied, as required by the Act which granted it." They therefore beg to be included in the schools named to receive the public bounty.

The other memorialists were equally insistent in their claim to receive a part of the school fund, as a matter of right.

The spirit and purpose of the Free School Society seem to be fairly represented by the following paragraph from a memorial addressed to the legislature at the regular session of 1824: "Your memorialists believe that this amendment of the existing law is recommended by many considerations of sound policy; and, among these, not the least is, that the interests of the whole Christian community will be best promoted by encouraging the principle that each religious society is bound to provide for the education of their own poor children, and that, if they attempt to do more, they ought to do it at their own expense, and not to look to the funds of the State for assistance" (Bourne, p. 69).

The minutes of the Common Council of the city of New York for April 11, 1825, contain the following item: "The Committee on Laws to whom had been referred the fourth section of the Act of Legislature relating to Common Schools in this City passed 19th November 1824 together with sundry memorials on the subject presented a report which was read and the consideration thereof postponed. It was ordered that three hundred Copies of the Report and fifty Copies of the Law reported by the Committee be printed in pamphlet form for the use of the Members" (vol. 53, p. 346, New York City-Hall Library).

The matter was finally taken up by the Council, April 28, 1825, and the law reported by the committee was passed. The first section of this law was to the following effect: "Be it ordained by the Mayor, Aldermen and Commonality of the City of New York in Common Council convened, Pursuant to the authority vested in them, by the act of the Legislature of the State of New York, entitled *An Act Relating to Common Schools in the City of New York*, passed November 19th, 1824, that the institutions, which shall be entitled to receive of the Commissioners of the Common School Fund, payable to and raised in the said City, are hereby designated to be, The Free School Society of New York, The Mechanics' Society, The Orphan Asylum Society, and the Trustees of the African Free School" (*Minutes of the Common Council*, vol. 54, p. 100, New York City-Hall Library).

The report of the Committee on Laws, to which was referred the act of the legislature, relative to the distribution of the school fund in New York City, and which was presented to the Council, April 11, 1825, as stated in the minutes cited above, is a document of the greatest importance. (The original copy is in the Custodian's office, New York City-Hall. There is also a printed copy in the possession of the Astor Library, New York City, and a reprint in the appendix to Bourne's history.) This committee heard both sides of the great question and its report gives a summary of the argument, which is invaluable to the historian. As to the fulness with which the subject was discussed in their presence, the committee reports as follows: "The various institutions, which have been established for, or have undertaken from the best of motives, the relief of this portion of our inhabitants (poor children), have been represented before your committee, and their respective claims to a participation in the public bounty, have been urged on the part of their delegates, by all the obligations and motives, which could be drawn from the sources of piety and philanthropy, and with all the force and energy of the most persuasive eloquence, and the most cogent argument."

The institutions in question, the report continues, are of two classes: the churches and religious societies, many of which maintain charity schools; and societies whose members belong to the various denominations and whose sole object is the gratuitous education of the poor, the chief of which was the Free School Society.

On behalf of the churches, the committee affirms, it has been maintained that their charity schools are of long standing, that they have enjoyed the fostering care of the legislature, that the children are taught the usual elementary branches with an efficiency comparable to that of the other institutions. It is emphasized also that in the church schools the children receive the advantages of religious instruction, and that for this the churches receive no compensation. It is urged also, in this connection, that religion is the only foundation of private happiness, sound morality, and capacity for public usefulness. They deny any intention of promoting sectarian influences, but affirm that no religious instruction can be given without taking some specific form or system, and thus, to some extent, becoming sectarian, and "that it is better to have a community of conscientious sectarians than a community of nothing-arians."

The advocates of the churches further insist that their schools, like those under the lay corporations, will be subject to constant supervision on the part of the city commissioners, that there should be no danger of a church establishment on account of the assistance they receive from the state, inasmuch as the rendering of such assistance is altogether different from endowing or intrusting them with public funds, without a specified object. No such danger, it was claimed, is felt by the general or state government from the habit of employing chaplains. They affirm also the impossibility of giving religious instruction in the homes of the class of children who attend the charity schools, that the trustees of the Free Schools are conscious of this and so teach the children under their care some religion: "but of that kind and in that degree which is calculated to meet the views of numerous and influential sects of christians." The delegates of the churches therefore contend that "this sectarian tendency, if it be an evil, is now kept within reasonable limits, by encouraging all religious denominations alike—whereas by placing its now divided forces, into a more concentrated form, its native intensity would be excited, and the consequences would be fatal to the body or association which it might infect."

On behalf of the lay corporations, formed indiscriminately of all religious persuasions, it is insisted, according to the committee, that the school fund, soon to become very large, should not in any degree be placed under clerical influence. The convention of 1777, or that of

1821, would never have sanctioned a proposition to tax the people for the support of religion, and the Common Council should now profit by their example and be guided by the same spirit. For the churches to participate in the public fund would be in violation of that prevalent rule of civil policy, which forbids all connection between matters of church and state. It is further maintained that a part of this fund is raised by tax, and that any portion of it turned into sectarian channels would compel one portion of the community, contrary to its wishes, to support the religious convictions of another portion of the community; that to pay teachers of sectarian schools from this fund in no sense differs from paying the clergymen of their congregations. When we are told that religion is taught in the church schools, it must be remembered that the catechisms and confessions of the churches are taught, and that these various creeds and dogmas cannot be all equally true and equally entitled to support. Preference therefore should be given the system which seems the best, and public support wholly denied all others. Any other plan would involve unjust and unjustifiable taxation. But no such discrimination is possible. The principles that would admit one to the public bounty would admit all alike. In this connection, "it is strongly urged that true religion requires and admits of no aid from the secular power; that her only resources are from Heaven and the contribution of willing hearts; that she seeks only for protection and not for support; and that the arm of the state, though strong, has no potency or legitimate control beyond such protection." It is further maintained that the school fund is purely of a civil character and should not be allowed to pass into the hands of any corporation not answerable to the civil authorities, and that it would be "a violation of a fundamental principle of legislation, to allow the funds of the state, raised by a tax on the citizens, designed for civil purposes, to be subject to the control of any religious corporation."

It was also contended on the part of the lay corporations that they caused to be communicated to their pupils reading lessons and catechisms, in the original language of the Bible, and such familiar aspects of human duty as children can best understand. Specific sectarian instruction is left to parents and churches and Sunday schools.

These are among the chief arguments presented by the lay corporations in opposition to the religious societies in order to prevent their participation in the school fund.

The attitude of the committee toward the subject referred to them is very sympathetically expressed in the following paragraphs:

"Your Committee have thus, with a single desire of truth, laid before the Common Council, the result of their inquiries, and the substance of the communications that have been made to them.

"In the performance of this duty, they have felt all the importance and responsibility of the task assigned to them, and while they would willingly have retired from the appointment, and do each individually wish, that the Legislature had passed the necessary law on this subject, on the recent application to them for that purpose, yet your Committee cannot permit themselves to hesitate or falter in the course of public duty, when that course is plainly manifest to their understandings. Your Committee will not conceal, either, their own private and personal wishes, at the commencement of their duties, that the well-organized churches and religious societies in our city, might be permitted to continue in the reception of a part of this fund as heretofore. But the weight of the argument, as urged before them, and which they have endeavored to condense in this report, and the established constitutiona, and political doctrines which have a bearing on this question, and the habits and modes of thinking of the constituents at large of this Board require, in the opinion of your Committee, that the Common School Fund should be distributed for civil purposes only, as contradistinguished from those of a religious or sectarian description."

The action of the Common Council has already been stated. The recommendation of the committee was adopted and an ordinance passed, denying the church schools any further participation in the public fund. This result had not been foreseen by the Free School Society when it took up the controversy against the Bethel Baptist Church. The problem involved in state support of church schools had only gradually taken shape in the minds of the people. The state legislature on April 8, 1801, had passed an act dividing the school money of the city among its different religious denominations to be invested by them, the annual interest to be used in the maintenance of schools. And there had been no question of the propriety of the charity schools under church supervision drawing from the public bounty. Without a challenge they had enjoyed this advantage from the first passage of the law in 1813. Nor was there any thought of the discontinuance of this mode of procedure until the controversy with Bethel Baptist Church was already far advanced. There seems to have been three stages in this awakening of consciousness. In the first place, on account of the special privilege granted them by the legislature, the Bethel Schools were working injury to the schools of the Free School Society. The first effort therefore was for the repeal of this special privilege. Apparently, as yet, there was no thought of asking the legislature to withdraw support from church schools. But Bethel Church contended earnestly for the vantage ground already gained, and other churches manifested a disposition to follow her example and to extend their school work beyond the borders of their respective congregations. This induced the Free School Society to take the second step forward, and to ask the legislature to limit church schools to the children of their respective congregations. It was just at this stage of the controversy that the Free School Society began to express the opinion that to allow church schools participation in the public fund had been a mistake from the beginning, that a fund raised for civil purposes should not be placed at the disposal of a religious organization. As the apprehension of this principle took definite shape in consciousness, the controversy reached its third and final stage. A strict application of the principle of religious liberty had prostrated the claims of the churches. The opinion of the law committee that the "Common School Fund should be distributed for civil purposes only" was enacted into law, and thus was completed the first chapter in the exclusion of religious education from the public schools of the State and City of New York.

CHAPTER VII

THE FINAL LEGAL STATUS OF SECTARIAN INSTRUCTION

Among the church schools excluded from the public bounty in 1825 was the Roman Catholic Benevolent Society. It was hardly to be expected that the verdict of the Common Council on that occasion would be accepted as final. Catholic persistence is too well known. We are not surprised then that six years later, March, 1831, the Catholic Benevolent Society applied to the Council for a part of the public fund to assist in the support of its Orphan Asylum School. Encouraged by this movement of the Catholics, the trustees of the Methodist Charity School presented a similar application later on in the same month (Bourne, pp. 124 f.). According to the proceedings of the Board of Aldermen, August 3, 1831, the ordinance of July 14, 1828, relative to the distribution of the common-school fund, was revived and re-enacted. The following amendment was also adopted with a majority of one vote: "To add to the number of Societies or Schools named in said law, the New York Catholic Benevolent Society; which additional Society shall be entitled to a portion of the Common School money, for such orphan children as are or shall be taught in the school, and maintained in the Orphan Asylum House, in Prince street, at the expense of said Society; and the said school be subject moreover to all the provisions, limitations and restrictions, recited and prescribed in and by said ordinance" (*Proceedings of the Board of Aldermen*, I, 256).

This enactment was then sent to the Board of Assistants for its concurrence, and was referred by it to the law committee. The report of this committee was received September 19, 1831, and attempted to deal with the constitutionality of the ordinance as passed by the Board of Aldermen (Board of Assistants, Doc. XXI, September 19, 1831). According to the report the constitution of the state, 1821, provides that the school fund "shall be inviolably appropriated and applied to the support of common schools throughout this State." The question then to be decided was, What is a common school? The law committee gave the following answer to this question: "A school to be common ought to be open to all, and those branches of Education, and those only, ought to be taught in it, which tend to prepare a child for the ordinary business of life. If religion be taught in a school it strips it of one of the characteristics of a Common School, as all religious and sectarian studies have a direct reference to a future state, and are not necessary to prepare a child for the Mechanical or any other business. No school can be common unless parents of all religious sects, Mohammedans and Jews, as well as Christians, can send their children to it, to receive the benefits of an education without doing violence to their religious belief.

"Your Committee cannot, therefore, find a more correct and accurate definition of the term Common School, than to call it a school in which nothing but the rudiments of an English education are taught to all who are admitted to it, which is open to every child that applies for admission, and into which all can be admitted without doing violence to their religious opinions, or those of their parents or guardians."

In the light of this definition the report of the law committee passes on to speak of the Roman Catholic Benevolent Society. It is considered to have strong marks of sectarianism about it. Regular membership in the Society is confined to Catholics, and its government is exclusively under the direction of that religious sect. And although the organization is open for the reception of destitute and unprotected orphans without any distinctions, yet all participants of its bounty "are exclusively instructed in the doctrines of the Roman Catholic Religion."

The constitution of the state, the report continues, guarantees to all mankind, without discrimination or preference, the free exercise and enjoyment of religious profession and worship. This is a recognition of complete religious freedom, so long as its exercise does not appear inconsistent with the peace and safety of the state. The appropriation of the public funds therefore to the support of the schools which teach the doctrines and tenets of religious sectarianism seems a palpable violation of the constitution. The attempt to raise by taxation a fund for the support of any religious sect would unhesitatingly be denounced as an infringement of the chartered rights of the people. But there seems to be no difference in principle whether such a fund be raised for the support of a particular church, or for the school in which the doctrines of that church are taught as a part of the system of education. In one case, a regular ordained ministry is paid for its instruction from the pulpit; in the other, teachers are paid for the same kind of lessons, delivered in a different manner.

It is the opinion of the committee that the school fund should be so disposed that all denominations, Jews, Deists, and unbelievers of every sect may derive the benefits thereof without doing violence to their consciences. It is poor consolation to be able to hold whatever religious views one wishes, while at the same time compelled to support doctrines to which one is diametrically opposed.

To admit asylums to the public bounty will, the committee thinks, open the school fund to any institution where children are taught gratuitously, and so to every phase of religious opinion and infidelity. This would be in direct violation of the principle established by the Common Council in 1825, denying participation in the public fund to all sectarian schools and institutions. The disregard of that principle now will give rise to a religious and antireligious party, and the union of the church and state will be fostered. Taxation for the support of religion is contrary to the constitution, and in violation of conscientious scruples.

So the committee reported the ordinance referred to it as unconstitutional, and recommended that it be so amended as to exclude from participation in the school fund all institutions not comprised under the definition of "common school" as given above. This of course meant the exclusion of the Roman Catholic Benevolent Society.

Nevertheless the recommendation of the committee was not adopted. The Board of Assistants concurred in the ordinance which had already passed the Board of Aldermen, and the measure became a law. The Roman Catholic Benevolent Society had won its contention. To this extent the law of 1825 had been repudiated, but the Council justified itself in the view of the public by urging as an exception the peculiar nature of an orphan asylum. As a verification of this statement, and so indicating the attitude of the Public School Society, relative to the question under consideration, the following extract from its annual report for 1832 (p. 6) is suggestive:

"It has again become necessary to advert to the strenuous and continued efforts that are making to obtain a diversion of a portion of the school tax from the legitimate object for which it is raised, to the support of church and sectarian schools. During the past year, the Catholic Orphan Asylum Society, applied to the Corporation to be admitted among the recipients of this fund. The application was opposed by the Trustees of the Public Schools, on the ground so often, and heretofore so successfully urged. Nevertheless this case was deemed an exception to the general rule, and admitted accordingly. The committee of the Corporation to whom the application was referred, [this was before the Board of Aldermen.] in their report on the subject, fully acknowledged the soundness of the 'cardinal principles' adopted in the law of 1825, which went entirely to exclude Church and Sectarian Schools from any participation in this Fund, but urged the peculiar character of an Orphan Asylum, as presenting a strong claim on public sympathy and support. . . . . The claims of an Institution so meritorious as the one in question, might have prevented opposition, had it not been for the pressing conviction, that the admission of the Asylum would induce others, under circumstances entirely dissimilar, to renew their applications for a portion of School Money. This consideration was urged upon the Corporation—but was met with the assurance that the full recognition of the correctness of the 'cardinal principles' established by the law of 1825, as set forth in the report of its committee, forbid any hope of success on the part of Church Schools."

The apprehensions of the Public School Society, relative to the probable activity of other church schools, were not without foundation. The application of the Methodists for their charity school had not been granted by the Common Council. But now, encouraged by the successful petitions of the Catholics for their orphan asylum, the Methodist Episcopal Church made application, in behalf of the orphan and destitute children attending the school under its management, for a participation in the school fund. This petition was on the point of being granted, when the earnest protests of the Public School Society came in to prevent its culmination (*Annual Report of Public School Society*, 1832, p. 7).

The position of the Public School Society in its opposition to the Catholic Benevolent Society is well defined in the address of the former to the public, giving the reasons for its remonstrances against the petition of the Roman Catholic Benevolent Society for admission to a common participation in the school fund (quoted in Bourne, p. 127). The petition of the Catholics is considered contrary to the fundamental principles of liberty and equal rights, and to the constitution of the state. The power of taxing the whole community is given for the benefit of the whole community, and so far as possible the benefits procured by such taxation should be enjoyed by all. The city corporation has no right to constitute a privileged class, however benevolent it may be. But the society in question is a closed corporation—its membership is exclusively Roman Catholic, and its beneficiaries practically confined to that denomination. Furthermore it is contended that the system of education at this institution is so combined with religious instruction as to deter, from conscientious scruples, many parents and guardians from taking advantage of the opportunities it offers. Notwithstanding these very persons may be taxed for the support of the institution in question. "But the objection to this principle extends much further; it embraces all, of every persuasion, who have conscientious scruples about paying their money for the support of any particular faith or who, if they have not such scruples, derive no benefit from the expenditure, and regard it as an abuse."

The further statement is made that while there were many reasons, in 1825, why one harmonious system of education, under the direction of one body of men, was to be preferred to "incongruous and irresponsible institutions," it was none of these that procured the victory over sectarian views, which brought about the revolution that eventuated. "That proceeded from the conviction that the school fund ought not to be diverted, in whole or in part, to the purposes of sectarian instruction, but should be kept sacred to the great object, emphatically called COMMON EDUCATION."

It appears then that, while the Roman Catholic Benevolent Society was admitted to a participation in the school fund, it was the orphanage plea that won consideration. The principle of religious liberty, so warmly advocated by the Public School Society, was admitted by the Board of Aldermen, and recognized by that body as still in force. The "cardinal principles" of 1825, denying to church schools the right of participation in the school fund, were still unchallenged by the law-making powers.

Nearly ten years elapsed before the attention of the public was again focused on the question of sectarian education. It was in 1840, when the Roman Catholics once more petitioned the Council for participation in the public fund in part support of their church schools. The annual report of the Public School Society, 1841 (p. 5), affords the following historical account:

"The hope entertained in the last report, that the efforts made by a religious denomination in our city, to obtain a portion of the school monies for the support of seminaries under their own exclusive management, would cease, the Trustees regret to say, has been wholly disappointed. So far from yielding to the emphatic language of a unanimous decision of the Board of Assistant Aldermen, and uniting in a magnanimous effort to extend the benefits of the Public Schools to the children of their own denomination, they again appealed to our municipal authorities. After a minute and careful examination of the whole subject by the Board of Aldermen, accompanied by a lengthened debate, thrown open to all parties interested, and a thorough examination of several of the schools, this application like the other was rejected by a vote, with a single exception, unanimous. Undeterred by these repeated failures, and apparently unconvinced of the injustice of the claim they set up, they have applied to the state legislature, for what they term redress, with what success remains yet to be seen."

The petition of the Catholics, together with the remonstrances of the Public School Society and of other societies and individuals were referred by the Board of Assistants to the Committee on Arts and Sciences and Schools. This committee reported on April 27, 1840 (*Journal and Documents of the Board of Assistants*, vol. 15, pp. 335 f.). The report affirms that on the part of the Catholics it was contended that the schools connected with their churches were established for the education of the poor connected with their respective congregations, although children of other denominations were not excluded. It was further stated that no religious tests were required for admission and that no attempt was made to alter the religious views of children of parents not connected with the Catholic church.

Objection was raised by the Catholics against the public schools. It was claimed that no religious instruction was communicated there; or, if any was given, it reflected upon doctrines of the Catholic church. It was further urged by the petitioners that they were taxed, along with other citizens in order to provide the school fund, and that they were therefore entitled to enjoy its advantages. They were however prevented from this for conscience' sake. Catholics could not send their children to schools in which the religious doctrines of their fathers were exposed to ridicule.

On behalf of the Public School Society "it was contended that any appropriation of the School Money, to any religious denomination for the purpose of educating the children of that denomination was foreign to the design of the Common School system, as organized by law, hostile to the spirit of the constitution, and at violence with the nature of our free institutions."

In the opinion of the committee there were two questions to be answered: Did the Common Council under existing laws have a legal right to appropriate any portion of the school fund to religious corporations? In the second place, Would such an appropriation "be in accordance with the spirit of the constitution, and the nature of our government?"

The Council has power, the report continues, to designate the "Institutions and Schools" which shall participate in the school fund.

To understand the meaning of this phrase recourse is had to a historical survey of public instruction in the city. It is the opinion of the committee "that the only authority under which religious societies participated in the School Fund, was contained in the act of 1813; and that this act was repealed by the legislature [November 19, 1824] with the full intention that religious societies, as such, should no longer receive any portion of the School Money from the Public Treasury, even for the purpose of supporting Common Schools."

In regard to the spirit of the constitution, the report goes on to say that the people of the state are divided into innumerable religious sects, each desirous of making converts to its opinions. In the old world this disposition had led to persecutions and martyrdoms, to the stake, the gibbet, and the prison. To prevent the recurrence of these abhorrent scenes in our own country, the constitution of the United States and those of the several states have in some form declared "that there should be no establishment of religion by law; that the affairs of the State should be kept entirely distinct from, and unconnected with those of the Church; that every human being should worship God, according to the dictates of his own conscience; that all Churches and religions should be supported by voluntary contribution; and that no tax should ever be imposed for the benefit of any denomination of religion, for any cause, or under any pretense whatever."

The opinion of the committee in regard to teaching religion in the public schools is stated in very decided language. This is what they say: "If religious instruction is communicated, it is foreign to the intentions of the school system, and should be instantly abandoned. Religious instruction is no part of a common school education. The church and the fireside are the proper seminaries, and the parents and pastors are the proper teachers of religion. In their hands, the cause of religion is safe. Let the public schoolmaster confine his attention to the moral and intellectual education of the young committed to his charge, and he fully performs the duty of his profession, discharges the trust reposed in him as a public agent, and fulfils his obligation as a citizen."

The report concludes by expressing the conviction that as the petitioners come before the Council in the capacity of a religious denomination, they have not, in that capacity, made out a valid claim to participation in the school fund. The intentions of the legislature, the expressed will of the people, and the requirements of the constitution all demand that the school fund be sacredly appropriated to "the purposes of free and common secular education."

The report just under consideration takes us a very decided step in advance of any position heretofore advocated. It is an unhesitating commitment to the policy of a "common secular education." Instruction in religion is "no part of a common school education," and if there be such in the schools, it should be "instantly abandoned."

It is interesting to note the changed attitude of the churches since the controversy of 1825. At that time they were opponents of the Public School Society and were more intent upon having their schools subsidized by the state than upon espousing any such abstract principle as religious liberty. The situation is different now. With hardly an exception they are backing up the contention of the Public School Society and are lifting their voices in protest against the diversion of the school fund. It was a battle of the giants. The Catholic churches were thoroughly aroused. Mass meetings were being held among the constituents of that denomination and wide excitement prevailed. (See speech of Hiram Ketchum before Common Council, printed in Bourne, p. 239.) It was their settled purpose to fight the issue to a finish, as may be inferred from the fact that when denied their petition before the Board of Assistants they turned to the Board of Aldermen, and, when again defeated before that body, they turned to the legislature of the state. They were contending for what they considered to be their rights. By paying their taxes they had made their contribution to the school fund. But they were not enjoying the advantages of this fund, because they could not for conscience' sake send their children to the public schools. They could see no reason why they should not receive a portion of the public bounty, and even based their plea on the principle of religious liberty and rights of conscience. (See speech of Bishop Hughes, reprinted in Bourne, pp. 202 ff.)

But arrayed against the Catholic petitioners were the Public School Society and many of the prominent churches of the city. These latter organizations had a vision now they had not enjoyed in days gone by. It was now evident to them that the granting of the Catholic petition would be a violation of the rights of conscience. They were now abandoned to the principle that public money should not be committed to the charge of any religious body whatsoever. In substantiation of the statement regarding the changed attitude of the churches the following remonstrances against the petition of the Catholics are called in evidence:

The Remonstrance of the Trustees of the Several Congregations of the Methodist Episcopal Church, March 6, 1840, heartily concurs in the policy of confining the school fund to non-religious bodies, and looks upon the granting of the petition of the Catholics as a perversion of that fund, notwithstanding the fact that on a former occasion they had petitioned for a similar privilege (*Journal and Documents of the Board of Assistants*, XV, 378).

The Remonstrance of the East Broome Street Baptist Church, March 25, 1840, regards accession to the petition in question injurious to the best interests of the community and destructive of the present popular and highly efficient public schools (*ibid.*, p. 382).

The Remonstrance of the Ministers, Elders, and Deacons of the Reformed Protestant Dutch Church claims that to allow the Catholics participation in the school fund would grant special privilege to one denomination and give it peculiar advantages of proselytism, and create an odious union between church and state. It would be in "direct opposition to a great principle of our government, and destructive of the present admirable and efficient mode of general instruction" (*ibid.*,p. 384).

The Remonstrance of the Ministers, Elders, and Deacons of the Reformed Dutch Church in Broome Street, March, 1840, declares that the petition of the Catholics calls for "an act, alike repugnant to common justice, the genius of our institutions, and the design for which the fund was created." Granting the petition would bring about two of the most odious features of a religious establishment: special governmental favor to a particular sect, and taxing the whole people for the support of a part (*ibid.*, p. 387).

The Remonstrance of the Consistory of the Reformed Presbyterian Church, April 7, 1840, affirms that for the Council to grant the Catholic petition would be "directly contributing to the support and perpetuation of the faith and practice of a particular religious sect; an act which would be at variance with the whole spirit of our civil institutions, involving a prostitution of the School Fund itself, and tending to create a privileged class in society, to the detriment of the others entitled to equal rights" (*ibid.*, p. 389).

It will not now be necessary to consider the application of the Catholics to the Board of Aldermen, as the issue was fought out before that body with the same arguments and on the same grounds which had been presented to the Board of Assistants. We can therefore pass on to the final stage of the controversy.

The defeat of the Catholics before both branches of the Common Council in nowise affected their convictions as to the distribution of the school fund. They were more determined than ever before. They were now nerved for the conflict. A central executive committee was formed, also a committee of two in each ward to carry out in the various localities of the city the measures recommended by the central committee. The Catholic movement, thus thoroughly organized, proceeded at once to hold meetings and circulate petitions (Bourne, pp. 350 f.). It was their intention to approach the state legislature, and thus invoke in behalf of their cause the intervention of the highest tribunal of the land. Its memorial was presented to the senate in the spring of 1841, which, together with the remonstrance of the Public School Society, was referred by that body to the Secretary of State, John C. Spencer, who made his report on April 26 (Randall, *History of the Common School System of New York*, p. 124). It was a very able and elaborate discussion of the relation of the state to religious and sectarian instruction. His fundamental position is that the state should extend education to all classes, that they may be qualified to exercise the duties and prerogatives of citizenship. The report in question has such great importance for our subject that it seems necessary to reproduce the following lengthy extracts:

"It is very true that the government has assumed only the intellectual education of the children of the state, and has left their moral and religious instruction to be given at the fireside, at the places of public worship, and at those institutions which the piety of individuals may establish for the purpose. But it is believed that in a country where the great body of our fellow citizens recognize the fundamental truths of Christianity, public sentiment would be shocked by the attempt to exclude all instruction of a religious nature from the public schools; and that any plan or scheme of education in which no reference whatever was had to moral principles founded on these truths would be abandoned by all. In the next place, it is believed such an attempt would be wholly impracticable. No books can be found, no reading lessons can be selected, which do not contain, more or less, some principles of religious faith, either directly avowed or indirectly assumed. Religion and literature have become inseparably interwoven, and the expurgation of religious sentiments from the production of orators, essayists, and poets would leave them utterly barren.

"Viewing the subject then practically, it may be regarded as a settled opinion in all schemes of education intended for the youth of this country, that there must be of necessity a very considerable amount of religious instruction. The Trustees of the Public School Society have probably no more in their schools than could be well avoided. While they profess, and doubtlessly sincerely, their readiness to omit everything that may be justly regarded as offensive, they yet maintain, and properly, that education is imperfect without inculcating moral and religious principles; and hence they allow the reading of the Scriptures or portions of them, and inculcate the leading principles of Christianity. But it is impossible to conceive how even these principles can be taught, so as to be of any value without inculcating what is peculiar to some one or more denominations, and denied by others. . . . . Even the reading of the text of our common translation of the Scriptures, is objected to by many, on account of its being, as they allege, erroneous and imperfect, while others deem its perusal by children, without explanation, positively injurious. Even the moderate degree of religious instruction which the Public School Society imparts, must therefore be sectarian; that is, it must favor one set of opinions, in opposition to another or others; it is believed that this always will be the result, in any course of education that the wit of man can devise."

This leads to the dilemma "that while some degree of religious instruction is indispensable, and will be had, under all circumstances, it cannot be imparted, without partaking to some extent of sectarian character." It is proposed to solve this dilemma by recourse to the fundamental law of the state, which guarantees "to all mankind" within its borders "the free exercise and enjoyment of religious profession." In harmony with this law no legislation had been passed by the state in any way connected with religious faith and profession.

"On this principle of what may be termed absolute non-intervention, may we rely to remove all the apparent difficulties which surround the subject under consideration. In the theory of the Common School law which governs the whole State, except the city of New York, it is fully and entirely maintained; and in the administration of that law, it is sacredly observed. No officer, among the thousands having charge of our Common Schools, thinks of interposing by any authoritative direction, respecting the nature or extent of moral or religious instruction to be given in the schools. Its whole control is left to the free and unrestricted action of the people themselves, in their several districts. . . . . The practical consequence is, that each district suits itself, by having such religious instruction in its school as is congenial to the opinions of its inhabitants; and the records of this department have been searched in vain, for an instance of a complaint of any abuse of this authority, in any of the schools out of the city of New York. . . . . It is manifest that the great source of the difficulties in the city of New York arises from a violation of this principle" (*Report of the State Superintendent*, January 6, 1842).

The report proceeds further to say that the Public School Society stands in the way of the direct management of the schools by the people. That Society, it is contended, engrosses the public education of the city, and makes impossible the action of small masses, as in the interior of the state. Under such circumstances the only possible application of the principle of non-intervention is by the total abandonment of all religious instruction. In a community composed of so many different religious sects no other method of procedure can hope to be acceptable to all. If, however, the degree and kind of religious instruction could be left to the choice of parents, in small masses, the chief cause of dissatisfaction and conscientious objection would be removed. The policy here recommended finds corroboration in the experience of twenty-five years in the school districts of the interior. This principle can be applied in the city of New York only by depriving its present system of its character of universality and exclusiveness, and by making it possible for small masses to give expression to their interests and opinions. In this way every denomination may enjoy its "religious profession" in the education of its youth (*ibid.*).

To carry out the suggestion of his report, Secretary Spencer drew up a bill, the purport of which was to extend to New York City the principle that prevailed throughout the state. A board of education was to be elected by the people consisting of representatives from each ward. This board was to have complete supervision of the system of public education in the city, and to act in co-operation with the Public School Society in the management of its schools (*ibid.*). But contrary to the expectations of the advocates of this measure, it failed to pass the legislature (Bourne, p. 426).

The Public School Society had not been inactive. It had strenuously opposed the effort to induce the legislature to modify the educational system of the city. Secretary Spencer's report and the measure he proposed met with its unqualified opposition. The reply of the Society and its friends was made through the Commissioners of School Moneys for the City of New York, who presented their annual report to the Superintendent of Public Instruction, May, 1841. Exception was taken to what Secretary Spencer had said about the necessity of public education being sectarian:

"In adopting a system of general education at the public expense, the object of the State was to give its youth such an education as would fit them to discharge the civil obligations of this life, leaving it to their natural and ecclesiastical guardians, to prepare them, through a parental and spiritual ministry, to render their account in another world. There ought to be, and there must be, some common platform on which all the children may obtain their secular education, who are destined to act as citizens of the same republic. To that general training, all the children are entitled; but it is the public who are to determine on its particulars and conditions, and not the parents who may claim it for their offspring."

The object of the school fund is to provide "for a civil purpose exclusively, not to prepare the path to any designated place of worship. . . . . This State has never yet asserted the power to tax its people for ecclesiastical objects; and if its sovereignty comprehended such a power, the rights of conscience require that the religion of the tax-payer be recorded on the assessment roll and his contribution be dealt to the encouragement of his own communion."

It will be seen from the extracts just gone before, that the Public School Society is occupying the same old ground. It is still making sectarianism the paramount issue.

In the following year, 1842, the matter was again brought before the legislature. This time the measure originated in the assembly. It was referred to the committee on colleges, academies, and common schools, which committee reported February 14, 1842. The report recognizes the complaint that the Public School Society has a monopoly of public education in the city. It considers furthermore that the public schools have failed to accomplish the objects contemplated in their establishment. A great number of parents are unwilling to intrust the education of their children to these schools, and nearly half of the citizens of the metropolis protest against the system and demand its modification. The remedy offered by the committee was in the nature of a bill, which contained the principal features suggested the year before by Secretary Spencer (Report reprinted in Bourne, p. 501).

The chairman of the committee, Mr. Maclay, of New York City, defended his measure before the assembly by saying there were only two classes of persons in New York as related to the subject—the one satisfied with, and the other opposed to, the present school system. To the former—largely the Public School Society—the bill proposed to leave schools as they were; to the latter, it gave schools under the same regulations as existed in other parts of the state (Bourne, p. 518). The bill passed the legislature on April 11, 1842.

The discussion of the school question before the legislature had one important difference from the consideration of that subject before the Common Council. Before the former it took a broader scope. There was a fuller recognition of the needs and rights of all members of the community. The Public School Society was a philanthropic organization worthy of the highest praise. Its record of benevolence was perhaps unsurpassed. But it seemed to fancy that its system of education was unsusceptible of improvement, and, while splendidly advocating the principle of civil and religious freedom, at the same time it represented a policy of mild coercion. It could not, or would not, understand why the Catholics refused to draw the water of knowledge from the educational cisterns which it had dug. But in the discussion before the legislature, on the part of the opponents of the system of education then prevailing in the city, sectarianism seems to have been forgotten, or at least suppressed. The necessity of providing for all the poor children of the city was the paramount issue, regardless either of Catholicism or Protestantism.

But the religious question was not omitted from the new law. For twenty years now it had been a matter of contention, of irreconcilable strife. The controversy of these twenty years at last finds a mandatory voice in the legal provision refusing all moneys to schools allowing sectarian teaching. The language of that law, so far as it appertains to our subject, will be of interest in this connection:

"An Act to extend to the city and county of New York the provisions of the general act in relation to common schools.

"Section 14. No school above mentioned, or which shall be organized under this act, in which any religious sectarian doctrine or tenets shall be taught, inculcated, or practised, shall receive any portion of the school moneys to be distributed by this act, as hereafter provided; and it shall be the duty of the trustees, inspectors, and commissioners of schools in each ward, and of the deputy (county) superintendent of schools, from time to time, and as frequently as need be, to examine and ascertain, and report to the said board of education, whether any religious sectarian doctrine or tenet shall have been taught, inculcated, or practised in any of the schools in their respective wards; etc."

Section 15. No school shall be entitled to a portion of the school fund "in which any religious sectarian doctrine or tenet shall have been taught inculcated, or practised, or which shall refuse to permit the visits and examinations provided for by this act" (*Laws of New York*, 1842, pp. 187, 188).

In 1843, April 18, the above act was amended. So far as relates to religious instruction, sec. 15 was modified by inserting immediately after "or practised" the following words: "or in which any book or books containing any sectarian compositions shall be used in the course of instruction" (*Laws of New York*, 1843, p. 294).

This provision, denying participation in the public fund to all schools in the city of New York in which there was taught sectarian instruction of any character, has been repeatedly re-enacted (*Laws of New York*, 1844, p. 494; 1851, p. 745; 1871, p. 1271) and was finally incorporated in the charter of Greater New York in 1897 (*ibid.*, 1897, III, 411), and in the revision of 1901 (*ibid.*, 1901, III, 491). But this restriction applies only to the city of New York. The laws of the state have been searched in vain for any general act relative to religious or sectarian instruction in the schools at large. There seems to be no such act. The decisions of the State Superintendent relative to this subject will be discussed in a later chapter.

CHAPTER VIII

THE RELIGIOUS CONCEPTION OF EDUCATION IN PROCESS OF MODIFICATION

The religious character of common-school education down through the first quarter of the nineteenth century has been quite fully demonstrated. It is the purpose of this chapter to trace, so far as the data will allow, the changing attitude of educational thinkers and of educational practice, relative to religious instruction in the public schools, for the remainder of the century. A good starting-point is afforded by *An Address from an Instructor to His Scholars*, pronounced at Woodstock, New York, April 14, 1804 (Samuel Pettis; in Astor Library, New York City). The author of this address was very probably the master of a private school, but his attitude toward religion is none the less illustrative of what must have been the prevailing custom in the public institutions of the time. It is gratifying to note that the instructor in question shows a very warm attachment for his pupils. He regrets that the time of separation has come: "Having labored for a considerable time in your education, received a compensation equal to my services, augmented by a laudable ambition in you, and finding myself unhappily arrived at a parting moment; I cannot feel my duty discharged otherwise than by offering you a few hints by way of advice."

He now goes on to address them on what he calls "the one thing needful," and here we shall let Mr. Pettis speak to us in his own words: "It is upon God, that we are dependent for every blessing; it is from this great source, that we derive life, breath, and every enjoyment; and it is owing to his beneficent hand, that we live in a country, where every material necessary to perfect the happiness of man, is profusely scattered in our way." Considering our material blessings and religious opportunities, "our hearts, if not adamant, cannot but feel a desire to bless his holy name, and are ready to acknowledge it the greatest ingratitude not to render him our thankful and constant services, for his goodness to us, and for those distinguished favors, which we are permitted through his beneficent hand to enjoy. I cannot conclude this paragraph, without calling upon you to seek the Lord in the days of your youth, before the stroke of death, to which, you are every moment liable, shall deprive you of that invaluable privilege. Follow, I beseech you, w th suitable humility the glorious examples and heavenly precepts of the divine

Philanthropist of Nazareth; which, when all the vanities of this life shall disappear, like an empty vision, will be the only comfort to make your passage through the floods of death, free from the most unhappy consequences."

Discussing the advantages of learning to read, Mr. Pettis says it affords us "the satisfaction of searching the divine volume for ourselves, which enables us from our own observation to become acquainted with our several duties to God and our fellow men." Continuing his discussion of the value of the various parts of the curriculum, we are informed that "astronomy . . . . is a sublime and useful science; it is well calculated to exercise the mind upon the greatness of the Almighty's power, in creating and moving the heavenly bodies, and is well adapted to humble the proud heart of man."

In the next place, the pupils are reminded of the duty of improving "the few remaining hours" allotted to their trust in such a manner that they may be able and willing to give an account unto God, having added to the measure of their talents to that degree, that they may receive the reward of "well done, good and faithful servant," and enter into the joys of immortality.

The address concludes by telling the pupils that they are now launched upon the tempestuous sea of life. They are therefore asked to take religion for their compass and director, truth for their pilot, love and contentment for their companions; they are to aim at the greatest glory of the heavenly Father, then with propriety they may look for the haven of perfect happiness in the world to come.

This schoolmaster could hardly be accused of holding the secular view of education. Nor, considering the evidence already adduced in the early chapters of this discussion, is it possible to think he was an exception to the general custom of his time. On this account he is introduced here, that we may be reminded of the thoroughly religious character of public education at the beginning of a century, which in the course of its passing decades witnessed almost a complete reversal of this earlier point of view.

The first step in this development, it seems, was taken by the Public School Society. From the first it attempted to make education religious without being sectarian. Its records furnish abundant evidence of this fact, and it may be well to present the matter in the language of the annual reports:

"The Trustees are aware of the importance of early religious instruction; and although the nature of their association and its true interests require that none but such as is exclusively, general and scriptural in its character, should be introduced into the schools under their charge, they require from the teachers stated returns of the number of their scholars who attend at the various Sunday schools or places of worship on the Sabbath" (*Annual Report*, 1827, p. 14).

"The Trustees have endeavored to keep in view the great object of the Society—the general diffusion of education, without regard to political or religious distinctions;—composed of persons of various opinions, they have permitted neither party, nor sectarian feeling to mingle in their deliberations, or influence their conclusions. Hence it may be safely inferred, arises the confidence which the community repose in the Society, and its Board of Trustees" (*ibid.*, 1831, pp. 2 f.).

"The constitution of the Society and public sentiment wisely forbid the introduction into their schools of any such religious instruction as shall favor the peculiar views of any sect, and the Trustees endeavor so carefully to guard them in this respect as to give no just cause of complaint, leaving this subject where it rightfully belongs, to the parents and guardians of the children. They wish however, not to be understood as regarding religious impressions in early youth as unimportant; on the contrary, they desire to do all which may with propriety be done, to give a right direction to the minds of the children entrusted to their care. Their schools are uniformly opened with the reading of the scriptures, and the class books are such as recognize and enforce the great and generally acknowledged principles of Christianity. A large proportion of our schools attend the various Sunday schools of the city, by direction of their parents, and the Trustees are happy to bear testimony to their great usefulness, believing them to be very valuable auxiliaries to the cause of public instruction" (*ibid.*, 1838, p. 7).

In confirmation of the claim of the Public School Society, as set forth in the extracts given, may be cited the words of the deputy superintendent of the county and city of New York in report to the state superintendent of common schools, December 31, 1842. This is his testimony: "Into the schools of the Public School Society, the fell spirit of sectarianism has indeed never entered. Their foundations have been laid upon the broad basis of christianity. In morals and religion, the Bible without note or comment, has from the first been their rule and guide, and standard. But catechisms, and sectarian books are rigidly excluded—the object being to sow the seeds and principles of divine truth, by a daily morning lesson from the sacred word" (*Report of State Superintendent for 1842*, p. 255).

These extracts need no further explication. They make plain the general attitude of the Public School Society. It believed in a general and fundamentally religious education, but eschewed all sectarianism as a thing impossible from the nature of its organization, being composed of various denominations; and as inconsistent with the genius of American institutions. But this was the first step in the exclusion of religious education from the public schools.

Another step in this movement was somewhat strangely taken by the Public School Society. This Society had championed the integrity of the public educational fund and had declared war against every foe of its sacred devotion to the exclusive ends of a common-school education. It had entered the controversy in 1822, when Bethel Baptist Church gave evidence of having unholy designs against the school money, and had hardly laid the armor down until the law of 1842 brought the matter to a final solution. The chief enemy during all this time were the Catholics and the slogan of the Public School Society was the civil character of the school fund and the sectarian nature of the Catholic schools. The Catholics were to be denied participation in the public bounty, because they were giving a sectarian education. But what if the Public School Society were giving a similar kind of education? What right then would its schools have to the fund sacredly set apart for the purposes of a common secular education? In their *Twenty-Sixth Annual Report* they had said that "funds raised by an equal tax, for promoting general literary education cannot, without a gross violation of the plainest rules of propriety and sound policy, be diverted from that channel, to propagate the dogmas of a religious sect, or further the interests of a political party" (p. 3). The Catholics were not slow to recognize their point of vantage, and so hurled against their great enemy, the Public School Society, the counter charge of sectarianism. The Public School Society, the Catholics said, was giving a sectarian education and therefore, according to its own argument, had no right to the school fund. In this way the burden of proof was laid upon the Public School Society. It must free itself of the imputations of the Catholics, and this it was found, could only be done by the expurgation of its school books.

This charge of sectarianism against the Public School Society was very boldly made in the course of the controversy of 1840. After the petition of the Catholics had been denied by the Board of Assistants, the former issued an address to the public, August 10, 1840. On the question of school books they make the following declaration:

"Besides the introduction of the Holy Scriptures without note or comment, with the prevailing theory that from these even children are to get their notions of religion, contrary to our principles, there were, in the class-books of those schools, false (as we believe) historical statements respecting the men and things of past times, calculated to fill the minds of our children with errors of fact, and at the same time to excite in them prejudice against the religion of their parents and guardians. These passages were not considered as sectarian, inasmuch as they had been selected as mere reading lessons, and were not in *favor* of any particular sect, but merely *against* the Catholics. We feel it is unjust that such passages should be taught at all in schools to the support of which we are contributors as well as others. But that such books should be put into the hands of *our own* children, and that in part at our own expense, was in our opinion, unjust, unnatural, and, at all events, to us intolerable" (Bourne, p. 335).

Just one month before, this question had been discussed in the *Freeman's Journal* by Rev. Dr. John Power, Vicar-General of the diocese of New York (reprinted in Bourne, pp. 228 f.). After discussing the objectionable character of the books used in the schools of the Public School Society and the attitude of that body toward the common-school fund, Dr. Power proceeds as follows:

"The objections to our claims to a due portion of the school fund are, I think, urged in bad faith. It is said that the State cannot lend itself to the support of sectarian principles. But recollect, sir, that this objection is urged by those whose conduct is truly sectarian, as far as regards the management of the public schools. This, I think, I have abundantly proved."

The Public School Society responded to these charges on the part of the Catholics by appointing a committee, May 1, 1840, to ascertain and report whether the books used in the public schools contained anything derogatory to the Roman Catholic church. A very earnest effort was made to secure the co-operation of the Catholic clergy in this movement, but without success. The trustees however persevered in their efforts and the final result was a very considerable expurgation of the textbooks used in the schools under their management (Bourne, pp. 325 f.). Their report for 1840 speaks of the repeated official offers they had made to expunge from the school books whatever might be objectionable, after thorough examination, to the most scrupulous conscience (p. 7). The report of the following year, discussing the dissatisfaction of the Catholics with the system of public education as then conducted, proceeds to show how the Public School Society had endeavored to remove every reasonable obstacle. With this end in view the trustees of the Society had resolved upon the expurgation of the school books of "every passage casting imputations upon the doctrines, practices, or characters, as such, of the Roman Catholic Church, or its members." But despite all this, they have to lament that the friendship and confidence of the Catholics had not been won to the public schools (p. 7).

Sufficient has been said, I think, to show that the charge of the Catholics against the Public School Society was not without foundation. There were books containing objectionable passages. This was frankly acknowledged by the Society itself, and the task of expurgation was industriously taken up. And the point for which we contend here is simply this: the work of expurgating the school books was another step in the exclusion of religious instruction from the public schools, not only because the books were expunged of all doctrines and tenets that pertained to the Catholic church, but because this movement on the part of the Public School Society marked a more decided commitment, in practice as well as theory, to the principle of non-sectarianism in education.

About this time another step in the movement toward secularism in public education, somewhat parallel to that just described in the Public School Society, was being taken in the state department of public instruction. The Superintendent of Common Schools, in his report for 1846 (pp. 46–50), gives rather a full discussion of district libraries, relative to the question of sectarianism. He reminds the trustees that, while they have the authority to select these libraries, they must exercise this authority under a standing regulation of the department of common schools, passed and promulgated when the law authorizing the purchase of libraries was first passed. The regulation in question discountenanced the purchase of "works imbued with party politics, and those of a sectarian character, or of hostility to the Christian religion." The report for 1846 then proceeds to call attention to the interpretation of the said regulation at the time of its promulgation. The interpretation reads as follows:

"1. No works written professedly to uphold or attack any sect or creed in our country, claiming to be a religious one, shall be tolerated in the school libraries.

"2. Standard works on other topics shall not be excluded because they incidentally and indirectly betray the religious opinions of their authors.

"3. Works avowedly on other topics, which abound in direct and unreserved attacks on, or defense of, the character of any religious sect, or those which hold up any religious body to contempt or execration, by singling out or bringing together only the darker parts of its history or character, shall be excluded from the school libraries."

The report goes on to speak of the full and free toleration of all phases of religious belief guaranteed in the constitution of the country. In accordance with this fundamental law, the prohibition, called for by the statute and enforced by the department, had not been intended to produce but to prevent injustice and to prevent majorities from encroaching upon the rights and interests of minorities. Individuals have the right to spend their money and devote their exertions, as they please, in order to propagate their religious faith and creed, but any such interference on the part of the state would wound the religious sensibilities of its citizens and violate a highly cherished principle of the fundamental law. It is the opinion of the superintendent that no work which, in the slightest degree, is sectarian should be allowed in the school libraries. The district library should be regarded as common neutral ground where all may meet divested of "offensive and defensive armor," and where the Trinitarian should not be denounced as idolatrous, nor the Unitarian charged with heresy. Furthermore it is the opinion of the superintendent that, if this prohibition be disregarded and the libraries made the receptacles of works of a controversial character, such marked public indifference would be encountered as to leave no hope of sustaining and perpetuating the usefulness of these institutions.

This ruling of the state superintendent was in line with the general movement away from the religious conception of education, which had obtained so largely at the beginning of the century. To all intents and purposes this was an effort to exclude sectarianism from the district libraries. So far as we know, the thought of the department of common schools looked not beyond such an immediate result. But, aside from the question whether there can be religious education after all sectarianism has been removed, the consequence of the movement in question could not have come short of narrowing down the thoroughly religious conception of education, so popular in former decades.

In his report for the year 1849 (pp. 221 f.) the State Superintendent outlines what he considers necessary for the improvement of the common schools. Teachers of the highest practical grade of qualifications, the regular and constant attendance of every child, the course of instruction systematized and extended so as to accomplish a thorough English education—all these are indispensable to the best interests of the common schools. Furthermore it is the opinion of the Superintendent that a sound and pure Christian *morality* should pervade all the teaching of the schools of the state. Education of heart and head must keep equal pace. Correct principles, right motives, and good habits must early be implanted in the youthful mind—"grow with its growth and strengthen with its strength." Too much care cannot be taken to make the influences of the elementary schools elevating and ennobling. To accomplish this, teachers of doubtful morality must be excluded from the desk and those secured whose "daily lessons and deportment shall inculcate and foster the great truths of humanity, integrity, conscientiousness and benevolence." There is no need whatsoever of any reference to denominational distinctions and sectarian differences. "The foundations of character, usefulness and happiness, may be laid in those enduring and comprehensive principles of Christian ethics and morality which lie without and above the pale of mere theology: and this is the province of the common school, so far as its means are adequate and its jurisdiction extends."

Alongside this declaration may be placed the decision of the State Superintendent of Common Schools on the right to compel Catholic children to attend prayers, and to read or commit portions of the Bible as school exercises (October 27, 1853). It is the case of Rev. Dr. Quigley, of Schaghticoke versus Margaret Gifford and others (see pamphlet in Astor Library, New York City). The complaint states that on the "8th day of August last, Margaret Gifford, a common school teacher in South Easton, Washington county, ordered William Callaghan, a pupil aged twelve years, 'to study and read the Protestant Testament': that on his declining so to do on the plea 'that he was a Catholic and did not believe in any but the Catholic Bible,' said teacher consulted the Trustees on the subject: that on the 9th of August, she again required the boy to 'read out of the unauthorized edition' [meaning King James's version]: that on his declaring 'his unwillingness to disobey the orders of his parents and violate the precepts of his religion,' the teacher chastised him severely with her ferule and then expelled him ignominiously from the school."

In discussing the question Superintendent Randall affirms his belief that intellectual and religious education should proceed hand in hand, but states that the realization of this ideal in the common schools of the country had met with serious practical obstacles. The government, realizing the necessity of universal education for the maintenance of civil and political institutions and not willing to rely upon the voluntary effort of individuals, had undertaken to organize and support a general school system. The common schools therefore were clearly a government institution, and to introduce into them a course of religious instruction conformable to the views of any particular denomination would be tantamount to a religious establishment. It was also impossible to formulate a course of religious instruction which would be acceptable to all, and to divide the school moneys among the various sects for the establishment of schools in which they might teach respectively their various creeds "would be, in the sparsely inhabited country districts, to divide the children within the territory convenient for attendance on a single school, and in which the support of all the inhabitants is frequently scarcely adequate, with the aid of the public moneys, to sustain a single efficient school into a dozen or more schools."

The following paragraph deserves to be given in the Superintendent's own words: "In view of the above facts, the position was early, distinctly, and almost universally taken by our statesmen, legislators and prominent friends of education—men of the warmest religious zeal and belonging to every sect—that religious education must be banished from the common schools and consigned to the family and the church. If felt that this was an evil, it was felt that it was the least one of which the circumstances admitted. Accordingly, instruction in our schools has been limited to that ordinarily included under the head of intellectual culture, and to the propagation of those principles of morality in which all sects, and good men belonging to no sect, can equally agree. The tender consciences of all have been respected."

The report of 1849 and the decision of Superintendent Randall, 1853, come to the same conclusion. The former considers that the province of the common school, in laying the foundations of character, is to inculcate the "comprehensive principles of Christian ethics and morality." The latter affirms that the logic of history calls for the banishment of religious education from the common schools, and admits only of the "propagation of those principles of morality in which all sects, and good men belonging to no sect, can equally agree."

In line with the conclusions just reached are all the subsequent decisions of state superintendents. We will let two of them speak here in their own language. In 1866, Superintendent Rice handed down the following decision: "A teacher has no right to consume any portion of the regular school hours in conducting religious exercises, especially where objection is raised. The principle is this: Common schools are supported and established for the purpose of imparting instruction in the common English branches; religious instruction forms no part of the course. The proper places in which to receive such instruction are churches and Sunday schools, of which there is usually a sufficient number in every district. The money to support schools comes from the people at large, irrespective of sect or denomination. Consequently, instruction of a sectarian or religious denominational character must be avoided, and teachers must confine themselves, during school hours, to their legitimate and proper duties" (circular on *Bible Reading and Religious Exercises in the Public Schools*, published by Commissioner of Education, A. S. Draper, 1906).

In connection with an important decision on the subject, Superintendent Weaver (in office 1868–71) made the following pronouncement: "The object of the common school system of this State is to afford means of secular instruction to all children over 5 and under 21 years of age, resident therein. For their religious training the State does not provide, and with it does not interfere. The advantages of the schools are to be free to them all alike. No distinction is to be made between Christians, whether Protestants or Catholics, and the consciences of none can be legally violated. There is no authority in the law to use, as a matter of right, any portion of the regular school hours in conducting any religious exercise, at which the attendance of the scholars is made compulsory" (*ibid.*).

These decisions, together with others to the same effect, were collected and published in 1906 by Commissioner of Education A. S. Draper. They may be considered therefore to represent the present policy of the Department of Education of the state of New York. They indicate the distance traveled from 1804 to 1906. According to these decisions and deliverances, formal religious instruction and the more obtrusive forms of religious motive are no longer to be given place in the schoolroom. An address from an instructor to his scholars, calling attention to their religious responsibilities and pointing out the religious value of the various branches of study, would meet with official censure. The highest school authority of the state has declared such an exercise to be out of harmony with the purpose and program of common-school procedure. Religious instruction and worship in the public schools of the state are now taboo.

CHAPTER IX

THE READING OF THE BIBLE IN THE PUBLIC SCHOOLS

After the legislature had enacted the law of 1842, denying the distribution of the public fund to schools in which sectarian doctrines and tenets should be taught, the controversy, from that time on, regarding religious instruction, centered around the reading of the Bible in the schools. It is the purpose of the present chapter to trace the development of this controversy and to take note of the changing emphasis of public opinion relative to the subject. We have already seen that the Bible was in the schools of New York from its earliest settlement by the Dutch and English. We have seen also that the law of 1842, while excluding all sectarian instruction from the schools, made no reference to the Bible question. It virtually left the whole subject in the immediate hands of the people of the districts and the officers they might elect to take charge of the local management of schools. It is therefore a matter of interest to understand something of how the people regarded the use of the Bible in the schools and something of the extent of its use during the second quarter of the nineteenth century.

We cannot feel that our information on this subject is complete, but such statistics as we have are worthy of consideration. In the year 1826 the New Testament was used as a reader in the schools of 168 towns; it was used in 216 towns in 1829; 200 towns in 1831; in 166 towns in 1832; in 124 towns in 1835; 101 towns in 1837; and in 109 towns in 1838. Just four other books had a wider circulation in the schools at this time. They were an *English Reader*, Daboll's *Arithmetic*, Murray's *Grammar*, and Webster's *Spelling-Book*. In 1838, they took precedence of the Testament in the following order: Daboll's *Arithmetic* was used in 457 towns, the *English Reader* in 437 towns, Webster's *Spelling-Book* in 227 towns, and Murray's *Grammar* in 209 towns (*Annual Report of the Superintendent of Common Schools of the State of New York*, for 1829, p. 58; for 1831, p. 71; for 1838, p. 147).

After the law of 1842 had settled the question of sectarian instruction, there was a decided effort to increase the use of the Bible in the schools. And this, in the first place, by official act. On February 7, 1842, Samuel Young was appointed Secretary of State, in which capacity, also, he served as Superintendent of Common Schools (Randall, p. 139). To an inquirer, some time in the year of his appointment (referred to in *Report of State Superintendent of Common Schools,* January 12, 1843, p. 255), he set forth his views on the use of the New Testament in the common schools. In this communication Superintendent Young expressed his regard for the New Testament as in all respects a suitable book to be read daily in the schools, and earnestly and cordially recommends its general introduction for that purpose. It has value as a reading-book, because of the purity and simplicity of its English, but he finds even a greater value in the moral influences it is capable of exerting. Education is something more than instruction. It includes the training and disciplining of all the faculties, it is the systematic and harmonious development of the future man for usefulness and for happiness. "It must be based upon knowledge and virtue; and its gradual advancement must be strictly subordinated to those cardinal principles of morality which are nowhere so clearly, and distinctly, and beautifully inculcated as in that book from which we all derive our common faith. The highest and most finished *intellectual* cultivation, in the absence of careful and sound *moral* discipline, can never accomplish the great end and aim of education. It 'plays round the head, but comes not near the heart.' It may constitute the accomplished sceptic, the brilliant libertine, the splendid criminal—but can never bestow upon mankind the benefactors of the race, the enlightened philosopher, the practical statesman, the bold and fearless reformer. The nursery and family fireside may accomplish much; the institutions of religion may exert a pervading influence; but what is commenced in the hallowed sanctuary of the domestic circle, and periodically inculcated at the altar, must be daily and hourly recognized in the Common Schools, that it may exert an ever-present influence—enter into and form part of every act of the life—and become thoroughly incorporated with the rapidly expanding character."

In no other book, he continues in substance, shall we find lessons of innocence, virtue, purity, and integrity comparable to those already endeared, we may hope, to the best affections of the children, in the New Testament. There is no more exalted standard by means of which parents and teachers may discharge their solemn responsibility of forming and molding the character of children committed to their care. The direction which the susceptible mind of the child may assume in the neglected district school may be fraught with consequences which shall bring about permanent advancement of society, or which may cast a withering and hopeless blight over the fairest prospects of humanity.

The communication concludes as follows: "But I have said enough in illustration of the paramount importance which I attach to moral and religious culture in our schools; and I trust no objections will be interposed to the general introduction and daily use of the TESTAMENT, not only in yours, *but in every other school in the State*" (quoted in Randall, p. 194).

It will be noted that this communication from Superintendent Young is not an order demanding the use of the Testament in the schools, but rather an earnest and cordial recommendation to that effect. Its actual introduction was intrusted to the disposition of the people in the local districts.

At the request of Superintendent Young in 1843, the Superintendent of Wayne County, P. D. Green, submitted a report on the use of the Bible in the common schools. It was published in the *Annual Report of the State Superintendent* for that year (pp. 667–69), and begins with the following interesting paragraph: "In the selection of books to be put in the hands of the young, the greatest care ought assuredly to be used. No book should be recommended until, not only its literary merits shall have been fully ascertained, but also its moral tendency and its probable influence upon the formation of the youthful character. In regard to the use of the Bible as a text-book, it seems strange that any objection should ever have been urged. Setting aside its moral worth, its literary merit places it among the first, if not the very first, of those books which it is proper to introduce into our common schools. There is no book extant so distinguished for its pure Saxon Language as the Bible. It may in truth be called a splendid exemplification of our mother tongue. Its style at once pure, clear and forcible, renders it easy of understanding, and fits it in an eminent degree for the use of the young. As a book for critical, rhetorical exercises, it would be invaluable. Its variety of style, its life-like delineation of character and simple narration of events, the clearness and energy of the didactic portions, and the unequalled sublimity of other parts, give to the Bible the highest claim upon the attention of such as would become thoroughly acquainted with the nature and power of our language."

In the next place, the report discusses the value of the Bible from the point of view of historical study. It is regarded as the only source of information for the three thousand years after creation. After this we are told that the highest value of the Bible consists in the fact that it is the word of inspiration from on high, containing precepts and instruction of the utmost importance to man as an accountable being. Such is the constitution of man that he cannot reach his proper rank and dignity on the basis of a mere intellectual education. His moral and religious faculties must be cultivated, and no book can afford such aid as the Bible. It is the standard in matters of religion, also of whatever is just and upright in character and sound in morals. The study of the Bible therefore cannot fail of exerting a highly beneficial influence upon the young. It should be read in the schools daily in a reverent and solemn manner. Teachers should show proper regard for it as a book of divine inspiration. In this way it will be greatly beneficial both to pupils and teachers. In corroboration of this view, Mr. Green refers to the opinions of others and says: "Very many teachers whom I have consulted have most fully acquiesced. They uniformly testify, that whenever the Bible is introduced and treated as the Word of God, its purifying and ennobling influence is seen both in teacher and pupils."

The report also calls attention to the value of the Bible for devotional exercises in the morning, and concludes with the following statement: "I would therefore suggest, that the Bible be recommended as a text-book for the more advanced classes, and that its general adoption in our common schools for purposes of worship, be strongly urged."

The two reports named above—that of Superintendent Young and that of P. D. Green, of Wayne County—recognize the value of the Bible for literary, moral, and religious culture, and were no doubt effective in the wider use of the sacred volume in the common schools.

The second influence making for the wider use of the Bible at this time is seen in the effort made to increase the moral value of common-school education. This was in the year 1843, and had its beginning in the special appointment from the State Superintendent of Francis Dwight, Deputy of Albany County, to report on the condition of moral education in the schools. After pointing out the great need of such education, Mr. Dwight proceeds to suggest how it may be effected. In part the mode of procedure is as follows: "The opening of the schools by the teacher reverently reading a short passage from the Bible, and repeating in concert with his pupils a few great moral precepts, relating to the various duties to parents, to each other, and to God, has become the custom of almost every school in this county. Its happy and powerful influence has been acknowledged by many teachers, discipline becoming easier and more efficient, and duty more cheerfully done" (*Report of State Superintendent for 1843*, p. 130).

The Deputy of Montgomery County, in report to the State Superintendent in 1843, urges the importance of moral education in the schools.

Not the social circle, nor the Sunday school, nor the pulpit can accomplish this work. At least, in his opinion, they have not done so. It is the moral principles of the Bible which he wishes taught, and expresses his great satisfaction with Superintendent Young's circular recommending the New Testament as a textbook in the schools (*ibid.*, pp. 435 f.).

The two deputies of Delaware County in their report to the State Superintendent, 1843 (p. 230), flatter themselves that there has been a decided improvement in the condition of moral education in the schools of the county within the past year. In their last report they regarded the schools of the county as exerting only a negative influence upon the morals of society. The Scriptures, and especially the New Testament, are considered the best system of morality extant, and a thorough acquaintance with the pure precepts of this admirable book cannot help, they think, but exert a beneficial influence in the formation of character. It thus becomes indispensable to the proper education of the children of this republic. In their first visits to the schools of the county, they were surprised to find that in very many instances the Scriptures were not even used as a textbook, and were not to be found in the schools. But at the present time, the report continues, they are used daily and almost universally, not so much as a textbook for reading exercises, as a book of standard rules for the regulation of conduct.

The Deputy of Livingston County, reporting to the State Superintendent in 1843 (p. 342), expresses his conviction of the necessity of good morals and the early inculcation of moral principles. Accordingly he had made it his duty to find out to what extent these principles were being inculcated and practiced in the schools. He found that the Scriptures were read in but few schools during the previous year. The past fall the matter was discussed at conventions, and, through fear of sectarianism, an attitude adverse to their introduction into the schoolroom was manifested on the part of some. This difficulty was obviated and the reading of the Scriptures secured by recommending to teachers that they be read without comment. He is now able to report that during the last summer (1843) nearly all the schools in the ten towns visited listened daily, as a morning exercise, to the reading of the Bible.

In this connection should be mentioned a state convention of County Superintendents, held at Syracuse, 1845. The following resolution was proposed: "Resolved, That this Convention regard the introduction of the Bible into schools as an object earnestly to be desired; but that the time and manner in which this object is to be accomplished is a question which ought to be decided by the inhabitants of the districts; and that in all measures for the promotion of moral and religious culture in our schools, sacred regard ought to be had for the rights, and tenderness manifested toward the scruples and prejudices of all." This resolution, with the modification that county superintendents urgently use their influence for the daily reading of the Bible in all the schools of the state, was unanimously adopted (Randall, pp. 200, 207).

All this time, however, in the City of New York, there seems to have been a strenuous effort going on to exclude the Bible from the schools. The law of 1842 had decided against all sectarian books and sectarian teaching, and the warfare against the Bible was now proceeding on the ground that it was a sectarian book. The report of the Superintendent of Schools for the City and County of New York to the State Superintendent, 1843, was a bitter cry against this movement. He declares it to be one of the unhappy consequences of the new law that "the Bible has been banished in several instances, while it has never been permitted to enter most of the district schools that have been organized." And while he does not wish to be regarded as holding the view that common schools should be converted into religious assemblies, nevertheless he thinks they should, in the broad sense of the term, be Christian schools, and therefore the banishment of the Bible therefrom cannot be regarded otherwise than striking at the very foundations of our school edifice.

Describing the actual situation, the report goes on to speak of one of the ward schools, where a large majority of the pupils were children of Catholic parents. The Douay version of the Bible, for a time, was allowed to be read on every alternate morning. But it was not long till the school officers of the ward yielded to the objections against both versions, and both were thus discontinued.

The report further affirms: "I have stated in my report to the Board of Education that the Bible was banished from the Manhattenville Academy in June last, upon the pretext, contained in a written order, that it is a sectarian book! In the same report I have enumerated the several district schools into which it has never been allowed to enter. The number, as compared with the whole, you will perceive is large" (*Annual Report of the State Superintendent for 1843*, pp. 415–17).

The report named above was made in 1843. The following year a pamphlet, entitled *An Honest Appeal to Every Voter*, was circulated in the City of New York (in the Astor Library). This brief document has value, showing not only something of the effort to exclude the Bible from the schools, but also how the question had become complicated with politics. The circular begins with exclamations of horror:

"This is the question! the great question! which, most of all, concerns the voters of this city, at the approaching election. All other questions are insignificant compared with this. Shall a foreign Pope, through his sworn vassal, Bishop Hughes, deprive our children of the Bible in the Public Schools? Let every American father and mother ponder this question.

"The deed *is done!* The Holy Bible *is* condemned! and expelled from *thirty-three* schools! and Americans and Protestants have been found base enough to buy up the *Irish Roman Catholic* votes, by tamely submitting to this outrage, and have themselves perpetrated this deed of infamy!

"The new school law, which has already taxed our citizens a Quarter Of A Million Dollars! for new schools, from which the Holy Bible is excluded, was passed at the dictation of Bishop Hughes and other Roman Catholic Priests, who it is notorious were closeted with Maclay and other corrupt and infidel politicians, when the law was framed thus to *rob our children* of the Bible in our schools!"

The report of the City Superintendent to the Board of Education is inserted at this point. It goes on to show that the Bible had been termed a sectarian book by the commissioners and inspectors of certain of the ward schools and that on this ground had been excluded from thirty-three of these schools. All this is regarded wholly contrary to law. The circular continues again:

"And now, fellow citizens of any and every party, if you have read this official report of the Superintendent of Common Schools for the City and County of New York, it becomes you to act at the coming election as if the *Bible in the schools depended upon your single vote.*

"Ask yourselves whether any *republic* ever existed or flourished without the Bible! Is *freedom* any where found upon the earth at the present hour, in any country where the Bible is a prohibited book? Can a child be educated for a citizen of America, who is not taught to reverence the Bible? Is there any sanctity in an oath in our Courts of Justice, unless the Bible is venerated as the Book of God? And whose property, liberty, or life would be safe, for a single hour, if men are not taught to regard the Bible with reverence and awe?"

The charge is made by the circular that the Democratic party is in collusion with the Catholics, and that to them, as a reward for their support, had been promised the exclusion of the Bible from the public schools. Voters are called upon to ignore party ties and cast their ballot for the best interest of their native land and for the Bible in the public schools. The circular does not seem to have been written in the interest of any party, but rather in behalf of the Bible in the schools. And though it may have been in the nature of campaign literature, the subject discussed must have been a point at issue, else the pamphlet would have been to no purpose. It seems therefore unquestionable evidence that, on the ground of being a sectarian book, the Bible was in some measure being excluded from the public schools of the City of New York, and that this movement was complicated with politics.

George B. Cheever, D.D., writing in New York City, 1854, fully corroborates the implications of the circular just described. He thus characterizes the political aspects of the question: "It is impossible, and perhaps it would be useless, in this place, to go into a history of the introduction of the Romish and political element into the management of a system of public education, that ought to be so high and sacred above all sectarian and political intrigue. We will not enter on the detail of the conflicts fought, the schemes presented, the influences used, the conferences of the school authorities with Bishop Hughes, the submission to his inspection of all the school literature for consideration, the disgraceful blackening of the school books by Romish expurgation, and the partial and temporary giving up of the school system to the dictation of Romish priests" (*The Bible in Our Common Schools*, p. 229).

As an illustration of the procedure which had for its object the exclusion of the Bible from the schools, the following written order from the trustees, served upon a teacher of New York City, will be instructive: "Sir By *unanimos* vote of the trustees Last Meeting all *Secterian* Books *is Requisted to Bee* Removed from the School as it is *thaught* the *Bibl* one it is *Requisted* to *Bee* Removed" (quoted in Cheever, p. 217).

The spelling, capitals, and want of punctuation in this order from the "trustees" do not very highly recommend the qualifications of at least some of the men who at this time were in control of public education in the metropolis of the empire state. It is nevertheless another link in the chain of evidence against the use of the Bible in the schools.

The report of the Superintendent of Schools for the County and City of New York, the pamphlet entitled *An Honest Appeal to Every Voter*, and the statements of George B. Cheever, all agree in the opinion that, consequent upon the law of 1842, an effort was made in the City of New York to exclude the Bible from the public schools of that municipality, on the ground of its being a sectarian book. But, as one might expect, this was only one side of the question. Fortunately we have a special report from the Board of Education, dealing with the matter from the point of view of that body. It is the report of the special committee on the communications of the County Superintendent, relative to the use of the Bible in the public schools of the city (in the Astor Library, dated December 11, 1844).

We are informed by this special committee that the superintendent in question had presented two reports to the board—one on October 30, another on November 13, 1843. It is claimed that he showed ignorance of the law defining his duty, and consequently had gone considerably beyond his powers, the climax of his arrogance being reached when he reported the schools of the fourth and fourteenth wards as having forfeited all claim to the school fund, because of neglecting to read the Scriptures at the opening of the morning session. The report continues: "Although the Bible is not read at the opening of all the schools, it cannot be said to be excluded from any one of them; any child may bring his Bible without let or hindrance. The ward officers are in no instance prevented from introducing the Bible into their schools, if they should think proper to do so. . . . . All that the friends of the Bible have ever asked from the State in its behalf, is that every legal obstacle to its free use may be removed and that the schools may not be prohibited from using it. The power of propagating the Gospel, with its sanctifying and hallowing influences, was never intended to be wielded by Legislative authority, in any form or under any circumstances." The report further continues: "It is the opinion of your Committee, that the use or non use of the Bible in the schools, is left by the law entirely at the discretion of the officers elected in the several wards, and the several societies and corporations who participate in the apportionment, and they are all at liberty to pursue such a course as their own sense of duty and the peculiar circumstances of their schools may dictate to them, as most expedient."

It was contended that the only authority of the Board in this connection was to withdraw the apportionment from schools in which religious sectarian tenets or doctrines are taught, inculcated, or practiced, or in which any books of a sectarian character are read. It was further maintained that comparatively there were only a small number of ward schools in the city in which the "salutary custom" of reading the Bible did not prevail. And these schools were made up almost wholly of Catholic children, whose parents hitherto had been unwilling to send them, and while sectarian teaching was not allowed, "Bible lessons and Scripture histories are among their class books." The Committee considers this to be a matter of congratulation, especially when it is remembered that "all the other schools in the city are permitted to enjoy unmolested all the advantages which may be derived from the public reading of a chapter in the Bible, once or twice a day."

The following resolutions were recommended for adoption:

"*Resolved*, That the Board of Education has no power under the present law to determine what books shall be read in the public or Ward schools in this city or county, that power being left entirely in the hands of the school officers of the several Wards, and the trustees or managers of the several schools or societies, who are authorized by law to share in the apportionment of the school moneys.

"*Resolved*, That the Board of Education do hereby recommend to the trustees and managers of all schools under their supervision, the reading of a chapter from the Bible, without note or comment, at the commencement of each of their morning and afternoon sessions, this resolution not being intended as a recommendation of any particular version of the Holy Scriptures."

It is plain to see that the Board of Education and the City Superintendent were not in accord on the question of reading the Bible in the schools. Apparently the Superintendent was a representative of the extreme Protestant view, which held that, at all hazards, the King James version of the Scriptures should be read in the schools. The Board of Education, whatever its political affiliation may have been, represented a more liberal view. It held, as stated above, that the use or non-use of the Bible was a matter that pertained to the officers of the district, and that they should determine from the particular circumstances of their schools what might be most expedient in any given case. Nevertheless the Superintendent "advised, counselled, recommended, and remonstrated, terminating his official labors by invoking the interposition of the Legislature" (quoted in Cheever, p. 216) to preserve the Bible from being turned out of the schools. In response to his efforts an amendment to the school law was passed, May 7, 1844, to the following effect: "But nothing herein contained shall authorize the board of education to exclude the holy scriptures without note or comment, or any selections therefrom, from any of the schools provided for by this act. But it shall not be competent for the said board of education to decide what version, if any, of the holy scriptures without note or comment, shall be used in any of the said schools; provided that nothing herein contained shall be so constructed as to violate the rights of conscience as secured by the constitution of this state and the United States" (*Laws of New York*, 1844, last part of sec. 12, p. 494).

This provision was also embodied in the act of 1851, to amend, consolidate, and reduce to one act the various acts relative to the common schools of the City of New York (*Laws of New York*, 1851, p. 745). It was likewise embodied in the charter of Greater New York in 1897, and in the revision of 1901. The subsequent laws of the State of New York have been searched in vain to find any modification in this statute. It is therefore presumed that the provision of 1844, relative to the reading of the Bible in the public schools of the City of New York, is still in force.

It must be noted, however, that the law of 1844 is wholly negative in its character. It confers no powers, but simply denies to the Board of Education the right to *exclude* the Bible from the schools. What was the occasion of this law is hard to ascertain, as there seems to be no evidence of any such move on the part of the board. Jurisdiction in the matter was left just where it was before—in the hands of the people of the districts. A former judge of the Supreme Court thus characterizes the act in question: "That statute, however, did not direct or recommend the reading of the Bible in the schools, but only forbade the commissioners of schools to exclude it, by such confused phraseology as makes it difficult of interpretation—enacting a *muddle* to quiet a *muss* existing between the Protestants and Catholics, on the subject of scripture reading in the city schools" (Hurlbut, *A Secular View of Religion in the State*, p. 32).

Reference has already been made to the state convention of County Superintendents, held at Syracuse, February 3, 1845. In a speech at this convention, on behalf of the Bible in the schools, Dr. D. M. Reese, Superintendent from the County and City of New York, declared that in spite of the recent law the controversy was still pending in the city he represented. On his last official visit to the schools, he found thirty-three of these institutions organized under the new law, from which the Bible had been excluded as a sectarian book. After representing these facts to the ward officers, and finding that they would take no action in the matter, he notified the Board of Education that the schools in question had forfeited their right to the public money. But these schools for the time being had continued to share in the public bounty. His next move had been to bring the subject to the consideration of a public meeting, at which over five thousand had been present. The matter was then brought before the common council, and an ordinance was passed, denying any share in the public money to all schools from which the Bible had been excluded (Randall, pp. 202, 204).

For the next ten years after 1845, according to official evidence, the reading of the Bible in the schools seems to have progressed without any considerable interruption. The Superintendent of Common Schools for the County and City of New York reported in 1850 as follows: "The practice of opening the schools by reverently reading a portion of the sacred Scriptures, is in general use. There are, however, some few exceptions—but in the schools where this good custom prevails, no one objects; and in the few where the custom does not prevail, they are not the more prosperous on that account. The common sentiment of the community is in favor of reading the Bible without note or comment, at the opening of the schools in the morning" (*Annual Report of the State Superintendent for 1850*, p. 120).

In 1852 the Superintendent of the County and City of New York, after speaking of the exclusion by law of all books inculcating sectarian dogmas, continues his report as follows: "The sacred Scriptures are not included in this category; and while the Board, at their discretion, feel at liberty to allow or disallow the work of any mere man, they would not use compulsory measures with regard to this good book, but content themselves by recommending its reverent use at the opening of the schools in the morning of each day. . . . . It is gratifying to observe that very few schools are without this book of books" (*Annual Report of the State Superintendent*, dated January 28, 1852, p. 131).

Again the Superintendent from New York City and County reports in 1855 that "with very few exceptions, the several schools are opened at nine o'clock A.M. by reading the Scriptures, after which the Lord's Prayer is reverently repeated by the pupils, after the teacher, and a hymn of praise and thanksgiving sung, accompanied by the piano; after which the pupils are remanded to their respective class-rooms" (*Annual Report of the State Superintendent*, December 1, 1855, p. 131).

But we are not to suppose that the reading of the Bible in the schools was now unchallenged. In 1854 a bill was introduced in the legislature for the daily reading of the Bible in the common schools of the state. In the remarks of Hon. Joseph W. Savage, of New York City, in favor of the bill (pamphlet in Astor Library, New York City), it is alleged that "we have heretofore, legislated in some measure to please at least one sect. We have permitted what any other nation in the world that recognizes the Christian religion, would never have allowed. We have suffered the Bible to be banished from many of our State Schools, have shut out from the children of those schools, the very book that all denominations of Christians make the foundation of their faith, and strange as it may seem, out of tenderness toward the consciences of a Christian sect."

In discussing this matter further, Mr. Savage continues: "We first excluded the New England catechism, this was yielded as soon as it was objected to because it was sectarian, and inculcated a particular creed. We then excluded all books in which there was any religious discussion. This was yielded for the same reason. We then excluded all books that spoke harshly of the Roman Catholic creed. Though this is a protestant country, we yielded that too. . . . . But we have done more than this, we have banished from some of our schools, some of the choicest English literature because it was offensive to the Roman Catholic taste. We have excluded impartial history because it spoke of the despotism of the Roman Church. We have mutilated books, and have blotted clearly authenticated facts, for fear of offending the conscience of this denomination or of exciting prejudice against the career of that Church in times long past. In this we have committed a grievous error."

The bill however failed of passage, as no record of it is found in the laws of the state. It was merely an episode in the long-continued controversy about reading the Bible in the schools, and is referred to here merely as evidence that the question was still alive in 1854.

An echo of this controversy comes to our ears again in 1858. In that year a pamphlet written by a "New-Yorker" was circulated through the city. It attempts to give a review of the school legislation of the state, and charges that the legislature had been hoodwinked by the Romanists, so as to pass educational legislation in their favor. It charges also that the Board of Education was under the control of the Catholics of the city, and that consequently the Bible was being put out of the schools. It is stated that by recent resolution of the officers of the Fourth Ward, embracing a district of forty thousand inhabitants, four school buildings, and fifty-four teachers, the Bible had been voted out of the schools of this section. It is the opinion of the writer of this pamphlet that the Board of Education had authority to enforce the reading of the Bible in the schools, and that the action of the ward officers was illegal.

The responsibility of this situation is laid upon the Romanists, and the voters of the city are called upon to change the personnel of the Board of Education. It is alleged that the Romanists have made the matter a party question, in order to keep themselves in power. A member of the Board, who was asked by the writer why he had voted against the Bible, replied: "I am not opposed to the reading of the Bible in the schools—only I had no time to see how my party stood on the question."

This writer, while reflecting an unsettled situation in regard to reading the Bible in the public schools, is, after all, extreme in his view. The Romanists were against the Bible in the schools, but they were not alone in this contention. The "New-Yorker" has not come up to the full measure of the principle of religious liberty. He does not seem to have sufficient regard for the rights and privileges of his Roman Catholic fellow-citizens (*The Legislature Hood-winked by the Romanists*, Astor Library).

This then seems to be the status of Bible-reading in the public schools of New York. For the state at large there is no legal enactment. And the special provision for the City of New York, to say the least, is considerably elastic in its nature. It confers upon the Board of Education no authority to introduce the Bible into the schools, but simply denies it the right of excluding the Bible and of determining the kind of version used. There were those at the time who contended that the law in question did empower the Board of Education to put the Bible in the schools, but the measure itself is plain, and such an interpretation can have no other source than the bias of partisan feeling. The real law on the subject seems to be public opinion. Whether or not the policy be sound, the legislature of the state has left the matter of reading the Bible in the public schools to the arbitrament of the people, and has conferred upon the State Superintendent only the right of an appellate jurisdiction. The inhabitants of the various districts, according to the conception of the law, were to be the governors of the common schools, and up to 1844, when the provision relative to the Bible was passed, there seems to have been no other thought than that the majority should rule (see Randall, p. 205). It remains now to follow in some measure the development of public opinion and to set forth the bearings upon the subject in question of the appellate jurisdiction of the State Superintendent of Public Instruction.

As a matter of fact opinion on the subject of reading the Bible in the schools has been divided since the beginning of the controversy in 1842. The best we can do therefore is to represent both sides of this opinion, with some intimation as to which side has grown in popular favor. The opinion which advocates the reading of the Bible in the schools is well represented by George B. Cheever, D.D. His argument was presented to the public, in 1854, in a book of three hundred pages

(*Right of the Bible in Our Public Schools*). Cheever was born in Hallowell, Maine, 1807. He was graduated from Bowdoin College in 1825, and from Andover Seminary, 1830. In 1839 he became pastor in New York City, where he remained a resident until his retirement in 1870. He was distinguished for his vigorous application of orthodox principles to questions of practical interest (Appleton's *Cyclopaedia of American Biography*). The opinion of Mr. Cheever is of peculiar significance here, because of his residence in New York City during the very years the controversy was so hot. He maintains that the Bible is being banished from the schools out of deference to the Roman Catholic conscience, and that this procedure means legislation against all other sects who reverence the word of God and desire its use in the system of common-school education. Such a prospect he considers altogether displeasing, and takes up his pen in opposition to the movement. His argument, as relates to the Bible, is condensed in a brief paragraph of the Introduction, which reads as follows:

"We propose to show that such a course [exclusion of the Bible from the schools] would be contrary to Divine law, and to all just and equal human law; contrary to the obligations of benevolence; contrary to the rights, and injurious to the welfare of the whole country; contrary to the principles of civil and religious freedom; contrary to long settled Christian precedent and custom, and to the expressed will, wishes, and judgment of the Christian community; contrary to our best local statutes; contrary to the decisions of the wisest statesmen, the most illustrious patriots, and the most learned jurists of our land; and contrary to the history and fundamental principles and provisions of our free school system, as established by the State and supported by the people" (p. x).

The contrary opinion is well represented in *A Secular View of Religion in the State*, by E. P. Hurlbut (Albany, N.Y.: Joel Munsell, 53 pp., 1870), and *Religion and the State*, by S. T. Spear, D.D. (New York: Dodd, Mead & Co., 393 pp., 1876). The former writer was an ex-judge of the Supreme Court of the State of New York. His opinion therefore is worthy of that respect which is due to the voice of authority. Not that Mr. Hurlbut's opinion is necessarily free from all objection, but simply that he speaks on the subject with the knowledge of a legal expert. He lays the foundation of his argument in the conception of the state. His view will be found in the following paragraphs:

"There exist but two pure, original sources of governmental authority: one professedly derived from the Supreme Divine Power, and exercised by divine right, which is theocracy; while the other is earthly and human, deriving all authority from the people, and is based on their consent; which is democracy. In the former the ruler is vicegerent of Heaven; while in the latter he is the mere servant of the people. The one is a minister of the Divine Will; while the other only executes the will of the people. The right divine is, of course, a mere assumption; but this assumption, believed and acquiesced in by a nation, becomes a reality, and, in general, a dreadful one. . . . . In a theocracy, the state is little or nothing—the church everything; or in other words, the church is the state; while in a democracy the state is everything, and the church is nothing, so far as law, or legal recognition is concerned. The church exists as the offspring of public sentiment, without giving law, or law given to it" (pp. 6, 7).

Again Mr. Hurlbut says: "Now in matters of state there cannot exist a more perfect contradiction than arises between the theories, on the one hand, that the church is everything and the state nothing, or only its mere instrument; and on the other, the state is everything and the church nothing, except a mere volunteer, to aid lawful authority by its moral and religious influence. A free and spontaneous religion may help to support the state, by the moral strength which it may confer on the citizen who is a pillar of the state; but the least drop of religion legally allied to the state, like the water in Father Tom's punch, spoils the state" (p. 7).

It is pointed out in the next place that the American government is a constitutional, democratic republic, founded purely on popular consent, and recognizing no source of power but the people. It acknowledges no spiritual power on earth and confines its ministrations to man's temporal relations. Its citizens as such are obligated only to be faithful to the state and just to one another. In religion they are left free to form their own opinions—it is a secret between them and their God. "All religious sects are equal and equally disregarded by the law. The citizen is not known as a religionist, but only as a man" (p. 8).

Applying this theory of the state to the reading of the Bible in the public schools, Mr. Hurlbut contends that the law of 1844, had it been perfectly consistent, would have excluded the Bible as a sectarian book. That it is a book calculated to arouse prejudice and strife is not a matter of speculation, but a matter of history. Already thousands have been offended and the path of progress strewn with the obstructions of fruitless controversy. Mr. Hurlbut sets forth his fundamental objection as follows: "The philosophical democrat objects to its introduction, because he would avoid the religious element in all matters of state concern, never forgetting, whatever his religious creed may be, that he is a member of a democratic, and not of a theocratic state. Whatever *he* may have personally, his *state* has no God, no Bible, no church, no religion. He sees at once the incongruity of the religious element in a state school, and would utterly exclude it. Certain men of science object against the Bible, that it conveys false notions of astronomy, and of the earth's geological history; and it is enough that they honestly so object, to make its use in the schools injurious, how ingeniously soever they may be answered by the clergy. Some men of culture and of elevated taste, do not perceive the great sublimity and beauty even in the poetry of the Bible, that is vaunted by its admirers; and although they might tolerate the book of Job, would by no means agree that the master of a school should read Solomon's song, or the fourth chapter of Ezekiel, to their sons and daughters. It is enough to make a quarrel that they so object, and a quarrel kills the school" (p. 37).

The paragraph above is supplemented by the statement that there can be no peace among the sects with the Bible in the schools. The Jewish parent objects to the reading of the New Testament. The Catholic objects to what he calls the Protestant version. And this is to say nothing of the friends of the "positive philosophy," the advocates of a progressive theory of creation, and the disciples of Darwin who, because they have no religion, may be considered to have no rights, and may thus be taxed to support schools in which doctrines are taught antagonistic to their beliefs (pp. 38–39).

We shall now proceed to state the opinion of Rev. S. T. Spear, D.D. (*Religion and the State*). His book is a thorough and masterly treatment of the subject. It conveys the impression that the author has met the issue fairly and answered the main questions involved with perfect candor and ample learning. There seem to be no distortion of facts and no juggling with words. And the opinion of Dr. Spear is all the more interesting and appropriate to our subject, inasmuch as he was a pastor in Brooklyn, New York, and lived in the midst of the controversy which he discusses in his book. His view of the functions of civil government, as related to religion, may be illustrated by the following: "Those who drew the plan of our National Government built the system upon the principle that religion and civil government were to be kept entirely distinct; and, for the most part, all the State governments are constructed upon the same theory. The general character of both is that they neither affirm nor deny any doctrine in respect to God and that they command no duty as a religious duty. They deal with the temporal rights and obligations of citizenship, without any reference to the question whether the citizen is a religionist or not. His religious faith is no part of his citizenship and no criterion of his rights. It confers upon him no immunities and imposes no disabilities. . . . . He is not forbidden to be an atheist and not commanded to be a Christian. He forfeits no rights by being the one and gains none by being the other; and as between these two extremes of opinion, the State does not undertake to decide which is the true and which is the false opinion. Such is the great American principle in respect to the sphere of civil government. This principle, being the exact antipodes of State theology admits of no reconciliation with it" (p. 117).

How the introduction of the Bible into the schools violates the "great American principle" is suggested in the following summary: "The result then that we reach from this analysis of the question is simply this:—that, by using the Bible in the public schools, unless the use be merely that of a reading-book, an American State, founded on the principle of the strictest impartiality towards all religious sects and of making no discrimination between them, undertakes to create and does create a religious establishment in these schools at the public expense, and after the Christian model, either Protestant or Catholic in its specific type, and to this end affirmatively determines all the questions and institutes all the agencies necessary to make it a fact. This, in plain English, is just what the proposition means, and what those demand who advocate it. The public school is what it is by State authority; and so far as religion is there, whether as a matter of instruction, or worship, or both, it is there by this authority, and there established by being included in a State school system" (p. 86).

Space will be taken for one more extract, with which we shall conclude the opinion of Dr. Spear: "The public school," he says, "is not a Church, or a synagogue, or a theological seminary; but a piece of State machinery, organized and supported for purely temporal ends—as really as a court of justice, a constitutional convention, or a legislative body. Its function is not to make or unmake Christians, or predispose children to this or that form of religious faith. It does not propose a *complete* education; and does not propose a *religious* education at all, either partial or complete. It proposes to do a certain thing, on the ground of its necessity and utility to the State, and to stop there, by not entering that field which lies beyond the purview of civil government. In short, it proposes a *secular* education, and that only—an education that would be needful and useful in this life, if there were no God and no future for the human soul" (p. 52).

The extracts given above from Hurlbut and Spear are in full accord. In their opinion the state is wholly secular, created only for the temporal interests of man, and should in no sense undertake the task of religious instruction. Complete separation of church and state leaves no place for the religious use of the Bible in the public schools.

It remains now to note what contribution the decisions of state superintendents have made to the legal status of the Bible in the schools. In 1871 (*Laws of New York*, 1871, chap. 461) by act of legislature, there was created a Board of Education for Long Island City, to have the general control and local supervision of the public schools of that municipality. That body proceeded to pass the following provision: "The daily opening exercises shall consist of the reading of a portion of the Holy Scriptures, without note or comment." Whereupon a threefold appeal was addressed to the State Superintendent of Public Instruction, Abram B. Weaver. The appellants were the Board of Trustees of the First Ward of Long Island City, and two private citizens of that city. The ground of appeal on the part of the board of trustees was that the enforcement of the provision in question compelled the pupils to be present at the reading of the Bible in the school, under penalty of expulsion in case of non-attendance at such reading, and that the regulation had been directed to be enforced against the protest of the trustees, many of the pupils, and their parents and guardians. In the case of the two private individuals, the appeal was grounded on the fact that their children had been expelled from school for refusing, in obedience to their parents, to attend when the Bible was being read.

In handing down his opinion, Superintendent Weaver takes occasion to say that the question involved in the appeals before him is not new in the school history of the state. Trustees had often claimed the right to enforce the attendance of pupils upon religious exercises in the schools over which they had charge, but that his predecessors in office, as well as himself, had uniformly held that no such right legally existed. Here he cites the decision of Superintendent Spencer in 1839, and of Superintendent Rice in 1866, and then proceeds to pass judgment on the case before him, as follows:

"The action of the Board of Education of Long Island City, in directing the reading of a portion of the Bible as an opening exercise in the schools under their charge, during school hours, and in excluding pupils from those schools, or any of them, on the ground of declining to be present at the reading, has been without warrant of law.

. . . .

"All persons, otherwise entitled to attend any of the schools of Long Island City, and who have been and are excluded therefrom for refusal to be present at the reading of the Bible therein, have had the right to be admitted to such schools upon the same footing as other pupils rightfully attending them; and it is, therefore, the duty of the said Board of Education to see that the right of all such persons, in that respect, is accorded to them" (circular on *Bible Reading and Religious Exercises in the Public Schools*, issued by Commissioner of Education, A. S. Draper, February 1, 1906).

This decision was handed down, June 5, 1872. Twelve years later, application was made to State Superintendent, W. B. Ruggles, for advice in regard to religious exercises in the schools of Orangetown, Rockland County. The application was from the Board of Education of Union Free School District Number Four, and represents that they "wish to move unerringly, but firmly, in the matter of sustaining the reading of Scripture and prayer as a part of the exercises in opening the daily sessions of our public school"; that they have "not required the children of non-Protestant families to participate in repeating Scripture or the Lord's prayer, but have simply required them to behave with decorum." It is further stated that a number of Catholic families "ask that their children be allowed to remain outside until the devotional exercises are concluded," and that "this interference causes much disorder outside of the room, and the subsequent entrance of these pupils causes a loss of time and disturbance to class work" (circular on *Bible Reading and Religious Exercises in the Public Schools*).

In handing down his decision Superintendent Ruggles refers to the constitutional provision of the state, guaranteeing to all mankind the free exercises and enjoyment of religious profession and worship. He then proceeds to call attention to the heterogeneous character of the population in reference to religious belief and the manifest impossibility of arranging a course of religious instruction for the schools acceptable to all sects. In view of this situation, he says: "The only alternative, therefore, to preserve the benefits of the constitutional guarantees, in letter and spirit, and to secure to all absolute equality of right in matter of religious predilection, must be, however reluctantly the conclusion is arrived at, to exclude religious instruction and exercises from the public schools during school hours" (*ibid.*).

He now refers to decisions of his predecessors in office. Hon. John A. Dix, 1838, is quoted as follows: "I have heretofore decided that a teacher might open his school with prayer, provided he did not encroach upon the hours allotted to instruction; and provided that the attendance of the scholars was not exacted as a matter of school discipline" (*ibid.*).

Superintendent John C. Spencer, 1839, having occasion to pass upon the question, made the following pronouncement: "Prayers cannot form any part of the school exercises or be regulated by the school discipline. If had at all they should be had before the hour of 9 o'clock, the usual hour of commencing school in the morning, and after 5 in the afternoon" (*ibid.*).

Superintendent Ruggles now continues his statement: "The principles laid down in these early decisions have been followed by every one of my predecessors in office, no distinction having been made between Scripture reading and prayers, but each having been held, in separate and distinct appeals, to constitute no legitimate part of the business of the public schools. They will be my guide and govern my action in all cases of like nature which may come officially before me" (circular on *Bible Reading and Religious Exercises in the Public Schools*).

This decision was given on May 27, 1884. It was indorsed in 1906, as well as all similar decisions prior to that date, by Commissioner of Education, A. S. Draper, and set forth as the settled policy of the Department of Education, in all matters pertaining to reading the Bible in the schools.

In regard to the authority attaching to the decisions of the State Superintendent, and the means of their enforcement, our information comes from Mr. Frank B. Gilbert, Chief of Law Division of the New York State Education Department. In a personal letter, December 7, 1910, Mr. Gilbert writes as follows: "The Commissioner of Education in this state exercises jurisdiction in respect to appeals brought to him by aggrieved parties from the action of the boards of education or trustees in the several school districts of the state. When a decision is made by him upon such an appeal it is conclusive. If in a particular case he decides that a board is wrong in requiring the compulsory attendance of pupils upon religious exercises which are established as a part of the school curriculum, his order is binding and may be enforced against such board by removal for failure to comply therewith or by withholding the public money from the district."

There have been no court decisions in the State of New York for the reason, it seems, that all appeals have been addressed to the State

Superintendent of Public Instruction. The decision of this department then must represent the legal status of Bible reading in the public schools, and they have been, as we have seen, uniformly against the use of the Bible, in these institutions, during school hours. The reading of the Scriptures, we are told, can "constitute no legitimate part of the business of the public schools." We conclude then that from the point of view of the principle of religious liberty, so ably represented by Hurlbut and Spear, and from the point of view of the decisions of the state superintendents, the Bible as a religious book is an outlaw in the public schools of the State and City of New York.

CHAPTER X

THE PHILOSOPHIC ASPECTS OF THE QUESTION

Recalling the argument thus far, it will be remembered that for about two hundred years after the settlement of New York what may be called common-school education was very largely religious, both in its ideals and in the materials employed. It was a conception brought to this country by the Dutch and the English, and is probably to be traced back to the fundamental principle of the Protestant Reformation. The priesthood of all believers called for the education of the masses. The individual must learn to read that he might be able to enter the temple of truth which was represented by the Scriptures, and there, without temporal or earthly mediary, worship at the altar of his God. This religious conception of education flourished in New York for about fifty years after the Declaration of Independence. About this time, as we have seen, the movement of exclusion began. In the controversy connected with the Bethel Baptist Church, which was terminated in 1825, the principle of religious liberty, as related to public education, was first clearly enunciated. There were those now among the people who apprehended that the school fund was purely of a civil character, and that to divert any portion of it for purposes of religious instruction was contrary to the spirit of our republican institutions. In 1842 this principle was embodied into law. Henceforth in the City of New York no school could participate in the public fund, in which religious sectarianism should be inculcated or practiced. In the country districts, as our study has shown, the matter still remained in the hands of the local school authorities, but it is hard to doubt that the situation in the metropolis must have exerted a potent influence throughout the state at large.

From 1842 down to the present time, the subject of religious education in the public schools has centered around the reading of the Bible. Opinion on the question has been divided, but it is believed that the principle of religious liberty has won an increasing number of adherents and advocates, and that in consequence of this and other considerations the number of those who oppose the religious use of the Bible in the public schools has been constantly growing. The only law on the matter applies to the City of New York, and is purely negative in its character.

It merely denies to the Board of Education the right to exclude the Bible from the schools. The real law on the subject is found in the decisions of the state superintendents. These, as we have seen, have uniformly declared that the Bible, as a religious book, has no place in the schoolroom. To say that the Bible may be read in the schoolhouse before or after school hours, as some superintendents have done, is wholly aside from the question at issue. The school authorities have no jurisdiction over those hours, and the fact that the reading of the Bible occurs in the school building, rather than in some place outside, is purely incidental. But the uniform decision of the state superintendents has been that the religious use of the Bible constitutes no part of a common-school education, and that such a use is therefore illegal.

In the meantime we have seen the character of common-school education undergoing a process of change. The religious conception has been abandoned, and in its place has come the notion of a purely secular education. This, however, does not mean an irreligious or godless education, but simply one that is free from direct religious instruction, and especially from sectarianism. In the broad sense it may be even more religious than it was in the days of the Primer and the Catechism.

Aside therefore from the law of 1842 precluding the inculcation and practice of sectarian tenets, and the subsequent amendment of 1844 denying to the Board of Education the right to exclude the Bible from the schools of the metropolis, we arrive at the following conclusion: religious instruction and the reading of the Bible have been officially excluded from the public schools of the State and City of New York. If they still remain in some schools, as they do, it is a survival of the old theory that this question is to be settled by the inhabitants and officers of the various school districts. But whenever objection is raised to this procedure, religious instruction, or Bible reading, comes under the prohibition of the state Department of Education, and is henceforth illegal. This exclusion of the Bible and religious instruction from the public schools has come as a result of an ever stricter application of the principle of religious liberty. The public school as an institution of civil government can take no part in religious instruction, but must forever be dedicated to the cause of common secular education. This has been the verdict of history in the State of New York.

We shall now proceed to inquire, in a brief way, whether this verdict is justifiable in the light of the prevalent conception of the American state and the ideals of religious education.

Writers on political science make a very proper distinction between the modern, and the ancient and mediaeval states. The ancient state was comprehensive. It embraced the entire life of man in religion, law, morals, art, culture, and science. There was no recognition of the spiritual freedom of the individual and ministers of religion were public officers. The Middle Ages recognized a dualism of church and state and symbolized the functions of each respectively in the spiritual and temporal swords. The mediaeval state was regulated by theological principles, and its ruler was the vicegerent of God. The church, which was symbolized by the spiritual sword, was considered to be higher than the state, as the spirit is higher than the body. It took charge of the education of the young, exercised authority over science, dominated kings and princes, and exalted the clergy high above the laity.

The modern state has become conscious of limitations to its rights and powers. It no longer claims control of religion, art, or science. Religion is left to voluntary initiative, and the priesthood is wholly an ecclesiastical office. Instead of being founded on theocratic conceptions, it is founded by human means on human nature. Instead of being regulated by theology, its principles are determined by the human sciences of philosophy and history. It feels itself independent of the church and makes no distinction between clergy and laity. It allows and protects freedom of belief and abstains from all persecution of dissenters. It delivers science from ecclesiastical authority, and regards the school as a civil institution, and leaves only religious education to the care of the church. (This comparison is based on Bluntschli, *Theory of the State*, Book I, chap. vi.)

The relation of religion to the state is, in a general way, defined by Bluntschli, as follows: "The modern idea of the State is not religious, but not therefore irreligious, i.e., it does not make the State depend upon religious belief, but it does not deny that God has made human nature, and that His providence has a part in the government of the world. Modern political science does not profess to comprehend the ways of God, but endeavors to understand the State as a human institution. All theocracy is repellent to the political consciousness of modern nations. The modern State is a human constitutional arrangement. The authority of the State is conditioned by public law, and its politics aim at the welfare of the nation (the commonweal), understood by human reason, and carried out by human means" (*op. cit.*, p. 61).

It seems therefore, according to Bluntschli, that there is to be no union between religion and the modern state. And whatever may be true of European countries, this view finds ample illustration in American politics. Here in theory and almost wholly in practice church and state are in separation. This of course has not always been the case. Colonial legislation exhibited many features of discrimination against various religious beliefs and professions. It was the multiplication of sects, the devotion to a common cause, on the part of all the people, during the perilous years of the Revolutionary War, and the general liberal thought of the times that brought forth on this American continent the principle of religious liberty in such perfection that we have not only religious toleration but religious equality. A writer of great ability thus speaks of the development of the secular state: "It has come out of the slowly accumulating experiences of mankind, as the political spirit has carefully and laboriously gone forward in its earnest quest for a government that at the same time shall be best for the individual and for society, that shall give the Church the largest possibilities and the State the greatest political efficiency. The Secular State is, too, the creation of religious men, who have persevered in their course with noble heroism in the face of persecutions, and who have worked with large views of humanity and in obedience to the manifest teachings of history to fashion a government where politics shall be free from religious hatreds, and where the Church shall be free from the despotisms and corruptions of politics. We may lament, we may denounce; but the Secular State is the expression and the outcome of a resistless tendency which will crush any man or institution that stands in its way and attempts to impede its progress" (Crooker, *Problems in American Society*, p. 211).

The constitution of this country, which, according to its own words, emanates from "the people of the United States," declares itself to be "the supreme law of the land." All the powers conferred and all the limitations imposed by this document rest upon the sovereign authority of the people. Its purpose, as stated in the preamble, was "to form a more perfect union, establish justice, insure domestic tranquillity, provide for the common defense, promote the general welfare, and secure the blessings of liberty to ourselves and our posterity." It is therefore a human constitution, devoid of theocratic taint and having in view only the temporal welfare of the people. Religion is wholly excluded from its scope. On this point there can be no question. The words of the constitution are decisive: "But no religious test shall ever be required as a qualification to any office or public trust under the United States" (Art. VI, sec. 3). And this declaration is supplemented by the first amendment: "Congress shall make no law respecting an establishment of religion, or prohibiting the free exercise thereof." What Spear says is therefore true: "The whole subject of religion is totally withdrawn from the jurisdiction of the General Government, not only by not being included in its powers, but by being expressly excluded therefrom" (*Religion and the State*, p. 210).

Turning now to the constitutions of the various states of the Union, instead of discussing them separately in their different provisions relating to the profession and practice of religion, we shall quote at length from a learned jurist of our country. Thomas M. Cooley, formerly judge of the Supreme Court of Michigan, gives the following summary: "He who shall examine with care the American constitutions will find nothing more fully stated or more plainly expressed than the desire of their authors to preserve and perpetuate religious liberty, and to guard against the slightest approach towards the establishment of inequality in the civil or political rights of citizens, based upon differences of religious belief. The American people came to the work of framing their fundamental laws after centuries of religious oppression and persecution, sometimes by one party or sect and sometimes by another, had taught them the utter futility of all attempts to propagate religious opinions by rewards, penalties, or terrors of human laws. They could not fail to perceive, also, that a union of Church and State, like that which existed in England, if not wholly impracticable in America, was certainly opposed to the spirit of our institutions, and that any domineering of one sect over another was repressing to the energies of the people, and must necessarily tend to discontent and disorder. Whatever, therefore, may have been their individual sentiments upon religious questions, or upon the propriety of the State assuming supervision and control of religious affairs under other circumstances, the general voice has been, that persons of every religious persuasion should be made equal before the law, and that questions of religious belief and religious worship should be questions between each individual man and his Maker, of which human tribunals are not to take cognizance, so long as the public order is not disturbed, except as the individual, by his voluntary action in associating himself with a religious organization, may have conferred upon such organization a jurisdiction over him in ecclesiastical matters" (*Constitutional Limitations*, 2d ed., p. 512).

Nothing therefore is more evident than that in America the principle of religious liberty is fully established. It is recognized in the state and national constitutions, and is therefore part of the fundamental law of the land. It is then not to be doubted that in this country church and state are separate and distinct. But religious instruction and Bible

reading in the public schools is a palpable violation of this principle. The rights of conscience in respect to religion are constitutionally guaranteed to American citizens. And for the state to undertake to do in the schoolroom what it repudiates in the church is to be guilty of a gross inconsistency. The exclusion of religious instruction from the public schools is the inevitable logic of that full religious liberty which the American state guarantees to its citizens.

Of course it may be a question whether the principle of religious liberty is a final solution of the relation of church and state. It were mere presumption to say that it is. What new light may come with the unfolding years, and what new and unforeseen situations may demand are all beyond the ken of human vision. We only know there is nothing in present conditions to justify the prophet of the future to speak of a certain day to come when religious liberty will be no more.

It is also a question whether the religious education of the children is not a matter of such great importance as to override the considerations of religious liberty. As a mere abstraction, of course, religious liberty is not to be contended for. But when we consider the practical worth of freedom of conscience in the lives of the people, and when we consider also that the religious education of the children may be accomplished by other means than the public schools, we shall not lightly set aside that liberty of conscience which has so slowly come to light through the lapse of the ages and which has cost such infinite toil and suffering. Indeed, as Professor Woolsey affirms, no other plan than the complete separation of church and state is possible in the states of America, "as long as all confessions are equal before the law, as long as freedom to found churches is open to all, and as long as the conception exists that a church is a spiritual body, acting on the state only by the moral and religious forces of individual persons" (*Political Science*, II, 467). Then, too, we have to remember that history is replete with evils resulting from the union of church and state. How else shall we explain the wars against the Albigenses and the Hussites, the Thirty Years' War, and the English Rebellion? This unholy union has forced unwilling compliance with ceremony and ritual, punished with death those who opposed the state church, refused Dissenters a seat in parliament, and denied them the right to take degrees in the universities. It has intensified religious hatred among the people and poured contempt upon all classes of Nonconformists. It has worked injury to the religious establishment itself, weakening the motives for religious activity, taking away the independence of the clergy, and making religious livings the gift of the state. It has exiled loyal citizens from their native land, has fostered hypocrisy by inducing men to sign articles of faith in which they did not believe, has given rise to the inquisition, and filled the earth with persecutions and bloody murder (see Woolsey, *Political Science*, II, 500). Surely men have a right to stand in dread of a policy which has wrought such vast iniquity in the world. Nor can there be surprise at the widespread feeling that it were better to bear the ills we have in the exclusion of religious instruction from the schools, than to fly to others which have been intolerably worse in the past and which promise nothing better for the future.

Alongside this view of the state we may very properly place the Catholic conception of education. Here so far as possible we shall let Catholic writers speak in their own words. Rev. Thomas S. Preston, writing in the *Forum* of 1886 (I, 161–71) under the title of "What the Catholics Want," thus defines the view of that religious body: "With us Catholics the question of education is a part of our religious duty. Our faith commands us to instruct our children in accordance with the principles of our creed. We are bound in conscience to do so; and if we are restrained from doing so, we possess not the freedom to practice our religion. If there were a law forbidding us to do so, we could not obey that law, since our consciences would demand that 'we should obey God rather than man.'"

He now proceeds to enumerate the various factors involved in Catholic education, and we are told that:

1. Responsibility of education falls upon the parents. They may use the aids Providence has given them, and must obey the spiritual pastors whom God has set over them. The state has no right to interfere here.

"2. We hold also that religion cannot be divorced from education. . . . . In the instruction of children we believe that it is our duty to teach them the truths of our faith while we open their minds to the light of natural science. It is our conscientious conviction that the elimination of religion from a course of education is really to inculcate atheism, and to seek to banish God, who is the fountain of all light, from the young heart and mind. Religion in education cannot be simply let alone as an unknown quantity. It must either be ignored, or fully taught, or partially taught." In the opinion of Mr. Preston, it should be fully taught, as one must believe that his creed is all true and in no part superfluous.

3. They believe also that morality, in the common acceptance of the term, is so bound up with religion that no moral principles can be taught without it.

He now proceeds to ask for the mode of accomplishing this end, and finds the answer thus: unite religious training with the education of the young. But the heterogeneous character of religious belief in this country precludes any common basis of instruction. This requires the exclusion of religious teaching from the schools. And there is, he thinks, no way by which this radical defect can be made up. The Sunday school is inadequate. The daily school is the only place that will satisfy the demands of religious education, but this institution has been secularized. So he continues:

"There remains then only one way by which the principles we hold sacred can be subserved, and the freedom to practice our religion granted to us. This is the establishment of denominational schools, in which from early childhood the truths of revelation and of the Divine law may be impressed upon the growing powers of the young mind. These powers will grow for good or for evil, for truth or for error. In this way every religious denomination would be able to provide for its own children, and to preserve what it professes to hold dear. And we will say that every denomination must do this, or be instrumental in its own destruction by the neglect of the most ordinary means of self-preservation.

"The public schools are godless. We say this with no intention of speaking ill of them, nor of ignoring their real merits. All their merits we appreciate. But they are, and must be godless, as neither the existence of God nor His revelation to man can be taught in them. They have only one end in view, and can have no other. This is the direction of the mind and all the impulses of the heart to the needs of time at the expense of eternity."

To be taxed for the support of schools not according to their conscience is regarded as a species of persecution. It is not just, he thinks, for Catholics to be taxed for the support of public schools when they cannot for conscience' sake send their children and when they are obliged to pay out heavy sums for the maintenance of parochial schools. This of course is nothing short of a plea to be relieved of the school tax.

The Catholic view of education is further illustrated by two extracts taken from journals of that denomination, published in the city of New York:

"We have no wish to see the common school system, that is, a system of public schools for all the children in the land at the public expense, broken up, and are quite willing to do our part towards sustaining it. We see no radical objections to its remaining with all its present machinery, provided that the schools for the children of Catholics be separated from the schools for Protestants or non-Catholics. Appropriate to the support of Catholic schools the proportion of the public money according to the number of children they educate, and leave the selection of teachers, the studies, the discipline, the whole internal management, to the Catholic educational authorities, and you may, in all other respects, in all prudential matters, let them remain, as now, under public control and management, and public boards, regents, commissioners, and trustees, if you will" (New York *Tablet*, November 27, 1869).

But this would be a parochial school at the expense of the state, and only a public school in name.

The second organ referred to above declares itself as follows: "The Catholic solution of this muddle about Bible or no Bible in schools, is 'Hands off!' No State taxation or donation for any schools. You look to your children, and we will look to ours. We don't want you to be taxed for Catholic schools. We do not want to be taxed for Protestant, or for godless schools. Let the public-school system go to where it came from—the devil. We want Christian schools, and the State cannot tell us what Christianity is" (*Freeman's Journal*, December 11, 1869).

The statements given above may very properly be supplemented from a more recent writer. Walsh, in the *American Catholic Quarterly Review*, January, 1904, in his article on "Religious Education in the Public Schools of Massachusetts," takes occasion to set forth the Catholic conception of education (XXIX, 93 ff., 116–17 in particular). In assigning the reason why Catholics have set up the parochial school, he says it is neither disloyalty to the state idea nor because the secular education of the common schools is insufficient. "But because in the common schools the State authorities have refused to give or to allow the moral and religious training that the parents of . . . . children rightfully and consistently demand. Because the education of the common school is not a complete education, since it ignores the most important part of all education, namely, of the soul. Because the idea of education in the common schools does not harmonize with the unchanging and unchangeable Christian idea of education. What is that idea? The cultivation of the child for life's destiny and life's work. *The child.* Not some paper doll or waxen plastic model, nor indeed the beautifully imagined darling flower or ethereal sort of creature that we hear so much about in later days, but the child of flesh and blood. . . . .

"The child cannot be divided and separated into physical, intellectual, moral and spiritual parts, except by a purely mental or metaphysical process that has no corresponding reality, but everything that happens to the child, from its first breath, is cultivating or educating the child in all four aspects. One part cannot be given to the parent, another to the street, and a third to the school, a fourth to the Church, but the whole child is cultivated by each one of these agencies, and the least lack of harmony between them in purpose or means has its effect upon the whole child."

The object of education is described as follows:

"*For life's destiny.* Once admit the Divine creation and Divine destiny the common non-religious school is bad, for as Ruskin once said: 'It does not tell the child whence it came, whither it is going and how to get there.' The whole view of education, of the value of one or other factor and method in education depends in a large measure upon one's conception of life's destiny. For the Christian there can be but one, expressed in those words of the Divine teacher: 'I am the way, the truth, the life. I am the light of the world. You are the children of your Father who is in heaven,' hence sons of God. *For life's work.* Yes, the school must teach the child the dignity of work, cultivate, for work, all the powers of senses, mind, will and soul."

Mr. Walsh closes his statement with the following summary:

"We plead for a school in which the atmosphere will be Christian; we plead for a school in which the teacher will be Christian and not neutralize, much less destroy, the influence of home and Church. We plead for a school where the books will be Christian in tone, spirit and substance; we plead for a school in which the Bible, as a book of revealed religion and the inspired word of God to mankind, may be read with note and comment and interest and instruction by one who believes in it as such."

Without commenting in detail on the Catholic conception of education just set forth, it is sufficient for our purpose to note that they contend for a strictly religious education, and that religious education from their point of view means Catholic education, instruction in the tenets and practices of the Catholic church. If such were the character of the public schools, Catholics would be the last to raise objection. But this cannot be, hence Catholics have asked to be relieved from the school tax, or to be allowed a proportionate share of the school fund.

And certainly it is no transgression of the rules of charity to say that this would be Catholic education at the expense of the public. But the chief point in the Catholic contention is this: their war against the public schools is in the last analysis a war against the character of the American state. It is war against that theory of the state, which looks upon its function as comprising only the temporal interests of man and which leaves all matters of religious profession and worship to the voluntary initiative of the people. A secular state, if true to its principle, can have only a secular school.

It remains now to consider the question of religious instruction in the schools from the point of view of the ideals of religious education. Religious education is concerned primarily with the end to be accomplished, the means and agencies are altogether of secondary consideration. It therefore does not unduly exalt either Bible reading or religious instruction, but places the emphasis on the development of character. In a general way, therefore, its ideals are comprised in the comprehensive aim of making Christian manhood and Christian womanhood. In the actual work of religious education it is necessary to distribute this aim over the various periods of growth and to state specifically what is wished to be done at each stage of development, but in every case the ultimate object to be obtained looks forward to the maturity and fixity of Christian character. It is now this broad aim of religious education in the light of which we propose to sit in judgment on the purpose and program of the public school.

At the very outset we are confronted by the charge that the public school is irreligious and godless. From the point of view of religious education this is a groundless accusation, even though there may be no formal religious instruction and no reading of the Bible in these public institutions. When we consider the large number of school teachers who are active Christians, when we consider the high moral and religious motives by which they are actuated and the invigorating school atmosphere created by their earnestness, it is impossible to believe that this charge which comes from Catholic sources is anything but a "windy suspiration of forced breath." The absence of formal religious instruction and the reading of the Bible no more makes the school godless than the absence of these exercises from the bank, the factory, and the store makes these institutions godless. An able writer hits off the situation in the following graphic way: "A shoemaker is not 'godless' because he refrains from pronouncing the benediction when he delivers a pair of shoes to his customer. Enough that his leather is good, his thread strong, his work thorough, and his promises are punctually kept. The same principles apply to a schoolmaster. As long as he does his proper work of teaching aright the branches of knowledge committed to him, and his intercourse with his pupils conforms to the spirit of Christian morals, there is no taint of profaneness to be attached to him or to his function" (Geo. P. Fisher, *Forum*, VII, 131).

It is gratifying to recall that, despite all the criticism derogatory of the public school, no one has yet thought to object to the presence of *religion* in these public institutions. The distinction is worth while. Religion is a life. It expresses itself on the manward side in the moral virtues. Now, however much we may withold our sanction from the program of theological indoctrination, there can be no objection to the exercise, in the schools, of love, sympathy, truthfulness, reverence, courage, and all the higher virtues of life. If then religion abounds in the schoolroom, we can afford, I think, to be reconciled to the inevitable fact that the theological indoctrination must be given elsewhere. If from the religious point of view there is to be any campaign for the improvement of the school, let the emphasis be here: more religion in the schools and not more religious instruction. In the meantime we can take satisfaction in the fact that, so long as religion is found in the schools, whoever charges them with being godless is guilty of misrepresentation.

In this connection some word should be said in defense of the view that the Bible should not be used in the schools as a religious book. There seems no escape from the conviction that the great majority of those who advocate the use of the Bible in the schools have in mind its religious value. They are contending for the Bible in the schools either as a symbol of religion, or as a manual of religious instruction, or as a book of religious worship. In this way they hope to create the spirit of reverence and impart the knowledge of religion. All this is supposed to be accomplished by the reading of ten or twenty verses a day, without note or comment. The purpose indeed is praiseworthy, but the method is inadequate. From the point of view of a thorough religious education, it is impossible to believe that such a use of the Bible can be attended with any great value. On the other hand it is easy to see how it may be nothing more than a worthless form, leaving not a trace of good upon the minds and hearts of the pupils. Religious education, which has in view the end to be accomplished and not the means, cannot possibly look with favor on any such procedure. And yet many of the advocates of the Bible in the schools seem to feel that their whole work is accomplished when once the sacred volume is introduced into these institutions. The suspicion is aroused that, perhaps unconsciously to themselves, they are looking upon the Bible as a kind of fetich, a book of magic power, that they expect its mere presence in the school to work the miracle of transformation. But surely they are leaning upon a broken reed. There is no justification for what they expect. The Bible is invaluable for religious education, but not such a use of it as they recommend. Religious education raises the voice of protest. It refuses to be satisfied with such a makeshift. It therefore has little to regret in the exclusion of the Bible from the schools. It believes that the school has suffered no loss and the Bible no injury nor insult. So long as religion abides in the schoolroom, it is content to have its symbol removed. Regardless of the means, it proposes to be satisfied with religious development, and refuses to call any institution godless which succeeds in making even a small contribution to such a gracious work.

We turn now to consider the question of what we have a right to expect of the schools, from the point of view of religious education. There must be no scoffing at religion, no ridicule of the church, no depreciation of moral and spiritual values. In no jot or tittle must they undermine the best influences of the home and the church. But it seems needless almost to make this remark, since there is not the slightest ground for believing that any such opposition exists, or is likely to exist.

We insist also that the aim of the public school shall be bigger than the intellectual. In this thesis a certain prominence has been given to the secular school, and properly so. But by such an institution we mean only a school devoted to the ordinary branches of public instruction, and in no sense a school dominated by materialistic ideals and purposes. A division of labor in the work of education has its justification. The public school has a right to recognize the limitations and restrictions placed upon its program of instruction. We cannot rightfully expect of this institution to give a complete education. But we do demand that it be conscious of its relations to the home and the church. While it may of right lay emphasis on the division of labor, it must not narrow its ideal to the limited sphere of its immediate operation. It should no more forget the agencies of religious education than these latter should forget the public school. In a word, while it may rightfully have in mind, a definite intellectual aim, it should hold in view the whole of life, and should therefore allow itself to be inspired by the moral and religious ideal, and should relate itself to all proper agencies for the cultivation of the higher life.

There are also some who insist that the public school should give instruction in what they call a common basis of religion. This being free from sectarianism, as they think, should meet with the approval of all. Aside from the question whether religious instruction reduced to its lowest terms would be sectarian, it cannot be forgotten that such instruction is still religious and that, as such, it comes under the ban of the principle of religious freedom. And, besides, such schemes are usually nothing more than feeble attempts to teach morality. It is true they insist that the existence of God should be inculcated, and this would be religious instruction. But what is the use of teaching public-school pupils the existence of God? They do not question it, and all we need to ask of the public school is that it shall give no occasion for denial of this religious conviction, but rather take it for granted in its method of instruction. (For such a scheme of religious education see *Proceedings of N.E.A.*, 1901.) The only value, in my opinion, of such schemes of instruction is the emphasis they place on moral education. We have, I think, a right to ask of the public schools that they seek first the moral development of their pupils.

In this connection also it may be insisted that the public school consider the claims of the Bible as a book of history and literature. This of course is not a religious question, and religious considerations can have no part in determining such a use of the Bible. It must be settled very largely from the point of view of the possibilities of the school curriculum in any given case. Yet we must believe that it is just as desirable to teach the history of the ancient Hebrews, as that of any other ancient people, and that such a course of instruction would be just as truly educative as a study of either the Greeks or the Romans.

And the value of the Bible as a book of literature is beyond question. In its finest passages it is unsurpassed by the world's greatest masters. Its literary range also is very wide, extending from the simple story to the profound and complex drama. It is therefore easily adapted to the interests and capacities of all grades. Such a use of the Bible will be free from most of the objections raised against it in the past. It does not involve exposition and interpretation, of which the different sects are so much afraid. In the hands of a skilful teacher it does not infringe on the prerogatives of religious liberty, inasmuch as the Bible as literature does not mean religious instruction, nor touch upon the grounds of religious belief. In short, the literary use of the Bible in the schools calls for no religious interpretation and no explication of theological difficulties.

De Quincey makes a distinction between the literature of knowledge and the literature of power. In this connection he thus characterizes Milton's *Paradise Lost:* "What you owe to Milton is not any knowledge of which a million separate items are but a million advancing steps on the same earthly level. What you owe is power; that is expansion and exercise where every pulse and each separate influx is a step upwards—a step ascending as upon Jacob's ladder from earth to mysterious altitudes" (quoted by Prince, *Educational Review,* II, 357). These words of De Quincey are pre-eminently true of the Bible. This book through the centuries has been a means of elevation and expansion and power. From this fountain the great writers of the ages have drunk, and through them, like waters of life, it has flowed out through many diversified channels and has thus been distributed in many parts of the earth.

Such a use of the Bible could not fail to be of great value to our young people, especially those of high-school age. There is no danger that the literary use of the Bible will lessen their appreciation of the sacred volume. The effect should be opposite. As Professor Moulton has said: "An increased apprehension of outer literary form is a sure way of deepening spiritual effect."

In conclusion we will consider briefly the religious opportunity of the public school and the contribution it is actually making to the higher life of the pupils. And from this point of view even the ordinary studies, such as reading, writing, grammar, etc., are not to be despised. They open the gateway to knowledge; they make accessible the experiences of the race, embodied in the great literatures of the world, and so make possible the enlargement and enrichment of life. And besides, there is an immediate interest and an immediate advantage to be gotten from these studies if they be pursued with diligence. If it be objected that this advantage lies only in the direction of moral development, the sufficient answer will be that for this period of life, at least, moral conduct is religion in action.

But the religious possibilities of the higher branches of the public school are beyond the region of dispute. Nature-study and elementary science bring the pupil face to face with problems which may become a moral inspiration and a religious incentive. The devout mind believes that God touches men through the earth and sea and sky, and all the forms of life. Such a study means a larger acquaintance with the realm of nature, and, while it need not involve any direct religious instruction, it should elevate mind and heart and fill the soul with the true and the good. As one writer has said: "The study of nature, in her wonderful and beautiful forms, is truly ethical."

Likewise history, biography, and literature easily lend themselves to the cultivation of the higher life. It would seem impossible for any earnest teacher to treat these subjects in the schoolroom without making an impression for heroism and truthfulness and righteousness. They bring the pupils in contact with the best phases of life and can hardly fail to exert a broadening, refining, and elevating influence. "In literature the true teacher has an agency that, rightly used, lends to the richest development of religious thought. The hope, the sacrifice, the heroisms and fidelities, that literature has enshrined in its most perfect art, form the subject-matter for religious inspiration to every earnest student" (*Proceedings of N.E.A.*, 1901, p. 547).

It is still a mooted question as to whether formal moral instruction should be given in the schools. But there can be no question as to the importance of cultivating the moral virtues in these public institutions. It is sometimes said that moral instruction gives only what the pupils already have, and therefore what they do not need. It is pointed out that religious and moral instruction in Germany have not produced the most gratifying results. So it is contended that the public school should cultivate moral sentiments and habits, and develop the moral nature of its pupils. And we must acknowledge that what the pupils need most of all is moral disposition and power, and that any scheme of moral education is a failure which comes short of this perfect work. However, a complete statement of the problem will include not only moral habits, but moral ideas and ideals. The cultivation of moral habits and the inculcation of moral ideas should proceed hand in hand. This makes conduct intelligent. But there is something higher even than a stock of faultless moral habits. It is the apprehension of the ideal. The ideal is the sun that illumines the pathway of life. Without it, however good the habits may be, life is in darkness and bondage. When, however, the ideal is apprehended, habits may be passed under review and modified as necessity may demand. Now, in this connection, the chief point is this: the public school affords a splendid opportunity for the cultivation of moral habits, the inculcation of moral ideas, and the discovery of moral ideals. The life and work of the school furnish occasion for the cultivation of moral habits; and biography, history, and literature afford the means for the inculcation of moral ideas and ideals. And these are all the more effective, perhaps, because incidentally and informally given. Such is the opportunity of the school in respect to moral education, and that this opportunity is being extensively utilized hardly admits of doubt. It is to be hoped, however, that in the near future there shall be no possible room for doubt.

Finally, it is believed the public school exerts a wide influence for good through the personality of its teachers. This is the most important factor in education. Religion and morality incarnate in the teacher are worth more than all else besides. Emerson well said, "It is little matter what you learn, the question is with whom you learn." It is impossible to exaggerate the personal agency. The following sentiments are fully indorsed: "The most potent of all forces is the personal life of the teacher. Young lives are easily molded and directed by the strong, earnest life of a Christian teacher. If our schools are taught by men and women of sound ethical and spiritual lives, devoted in the most conscientious way to the work of building up in the children the highest elements of worthy manhood and noble womanly character, shall we not have met the most important condition of religious education?" (*Proceedings of N.E.A.*, 1901, p. 548).

It must therefore be freely acknowledged that the public school is a very important ally in the work of religious education. Its contribution to this worthy end is not to be despised. Yet, after all, the public school has its severe limitations. As we have said, it cannot give a complete training. The great burden of religious education still rests upon the agencies of the home and the church, and there is no prospect that this burden will soon be shifted to other shoulders. Neither the church nor the home can escape its tremendous task, its gigantic responsibility. May there be no shirking of the task, no evasion of the responsibility! Nay, rather let this demand be met with large equipment, with ample intelligence, with unfailing courage, and with passionate devotion.

www.ingramcontent.com/pod-product-compliance
Lightning Source LLC
LaVergne TN
LVHW021423110826
845150LV00007B/2062

* 9 7 8 1 4 2 5 5 0 9 1 9 4 *